Jane Eyre

CHARLOTTE BRONTË

Oxford Literature Companions

Notes and activities: Alison Smith
Series consultant: Peter Buckroyd

OXFORD
UNIVERSITY PRESS

Contents

What are Oxford Literature Companions?

Oxford Literature Companions is a series designed to provide you with comprehensive support for popular set texts. You can use the Companion alongside your novel, using relevant sections during your studies or using the book as a whole for revision.

Each Companion includes detailed guidance and practical activities on:

- **Plot and Structure**
- **Context**
- **Characters**
- **Language**
- **Themes**
- **Skills and Practice**

How does this book help with exam preparation?

As well as providing guidance on key areas of the novel, throughout this book you will also find 'Upgrade' features. These are tips to help with your exam preparation and performance.

In addition, in the extensive **Skills and Practice** chapter, the 'Preparing for your assessment' section provides detailed guidance on areas such as how to prepare for the exam, understanding the question, planning your response and hints for what to do (or not do) in the exam.

In the **Skills and Practice** chapter there is also a bank of **Sample questions** and **Sample answers**. The **Sample answers** are marked and include annotations and a summative comment.

How does this book help with terminology?

Throughout the book, key terms are **highlighted** in the text and explained on the same page. There is also a detailed **Glossary** at the end of the book that explains, in the context of the novel, all the relevant literary terms highlighted in this book.

Which edition of the novel has this book used?

Quotations have been taken from the Oxford University Press edition of Jane Eyre (9780198355328). This edition restarts chapter numbering at the beginning of each volume. Other editions refer to chapters consecutively throughout the novel. If using one of these editions, the chart below can be used to convert the chapter number references in this Oxford Literature Companion:

	Chapter numbers														
Volume 1	1	2	3	4	5	6	7	8	9	10	11	12	13	14	15
	1	2	3	4	5	6	7	8	9	10	11	12	13	14	15
Volume 2	1	2	3	4	5	6	7	8	9	10	11				
	16	17	18	19	20	21	22	23	24	25	26				
Volume 3	1	2	3	4	5	6	7	8	9	10	11	12			
	27	28	29	30	31	32	33	34	35	36	37	38			

How does this book work?

Each book in the Oxford Literature Companions series follows the same approach and includes the following features:

- **Key quotations** from the novel
- **Key terms** explained on the page and linked to a complete glossary at the end of the book
- **Activity boxes** to help improve your understanding of the text
- **Upgrade** tips to help prepare you for your assessment

Plot

Volume 1, Chapter 1

The novel opens with the **narrator**, who we later discover is the **eponymous** Jane Eyre, explaining that she lives with her aunt Mrs Reed, and her cousins Eliza, John and Georgiana. She is being punished by her aunt, but Jane doesn't really understand what she has done wrong.

Her punishment is to be isolated from the rest of the family, and she hides in the drawing room to read, saying that, with a book **'I was then happy: happy at least in my way. I feared nothing but interruption'**.

John comes to find her, and Jane explains that he disliked her. He is deliberately cruel to the ten-year-old Jane, mocking her for being an orphan. He throws the book that she was reading at her, and she falls and hurts her head. When she retaliates, he attacks her.

At the end of the chapter, it is Jane who is punished, as her aunt orders the servants to lock her in the red room.

- It is clear from the start that Jane is not considered to be part of the Reed family. She is **'humbled by the consciousness of my physical inferiority to Eliza, John, and Georgiana Reed'** and is excluded from the group around the fire.
- The account of Jane's reading suggests that she is a highly imaginative child, and her reference to having **'read Goldsmith's History of Rome'** shows that she is also intelligent and informed.
- This is a **retrospective** account. The adult Jane reflects on the imperfect memories from childhood.

Volume 1, Chapter 2

Jane resists being taken to the red room and is threatened with being tied down. She describes the room and reveals that this is the room where her late uncle died.

Time passes and darkness begins to fall. Jane begins to fear that the ghost of her dead uncle is coming to get her, and she screams in fright. The servants come to see what is wrong but Mrs Reed says that she is trying to avoid her punishment and insists that she stays another hour. At the end of the chapter, she faints.

Jane is overtaken by fear when she is locked in the red room

- As she remains locked in the room, she thinks about her position in the family, and describes her cousins in detail.
- The sense of Jane's fright grows over the course of the chapter.
- Looking back as an adult, Jane can see that her aunt saw her as **'a compound of virulent passions, mean spirit, and dangerous duplicity'**.

Key quotations

"[...] you are under obligations to Mrs. Reed: she keeps you; if she were to turn you off, you would have to go to the poor-house."

Why was I always suffering, always brow-beaten, always accused, for ever condemned? Why could I never please? Why was it useless to try to win any one's favour?

Activity 1

Look at the description of the red room which begins 'The red-room was a spare chamber' and ends 'I returned to my stool'.

- What is your first impression of the room from this description?
- What does her description of the room suggest to us about Jane's character?

Volume 1, Chapter 3

When Jane comes round, an **apothecary** is taking care of her. Bessie, a maid, shows her some compassion by agreeing to sleep in the nursery with her. Jane stays awake because she is so afraid of what she thought she saw.

The following day, Mr Lloyd, the apothecary, comes back and asks her why she is so miserable. She says that it is because she has no family. When he asks if she would like to go to school, she says yes because she sees it as a means of escape: 'school would be a complete change: it implied a long journey, an entire separation from Gateshead, an entrance into a new life'.

- Jane reveals that she has some quite snobbish views about **class**, possibly because of the way in which the Reeds have brought her up. She thinks that poor people are somehow inferior: 'I could not see how poor people had the means of being kind'.

Volume 1, Chapter 4

Time passes. Mrs Reed ignores Jane more and more, and it is clear that she has told the children to avoid her too. John attempts to tell her off, but Jane fights back.

apothecary a type of doctor who treated people for free

class the social group that people belonged to

eponymous the person the novel is named after

narrator the person telling the story

retrospective looking back

After Christmas, Jane is finally told that she is going to school. She meets Mr Brocklehurst, the master of Lowood School, who has come to inspect her. Mrs Reed tells him that Jane has "a tendency to deceit".

- Mr Brocklehurst's description of Lowood suggests that it is a place designed to teach poor children what is expected of them by society: that they should know their place.
- Jane's replies to Mr Brocklehurst's questions about heaven and hell suggest that she is not familiar with the Bible, but also suggest that she is critical of his version of Christianity.
- Mr Brocklehurst agrees to take Jane, and says that he will collect her in a couple of weeks. Left alone with her aunt, Jane finally tells her what she thinks of her, which shocks her aunt greatly.
- Jane reveals the human capacity for love in the way in which she talks about her doll: 'human beings must love something, and, in the dearth of worthier objects of affection, I contrived to find a pleasure in loving and cherishing a faded **graven image**, shabby as a miniature scarecrow'.
- Looking back, Jane shows some understanding of why her aunt behaved as she did, although she cannot forgive her for it.

Volume 1, Chapter 5

On the day that she is to leave, Jane is up very early. She makes the journey to Lowood School alone and arrives when it is already dark. She is so tired and excited that she can't eat anything at the evening meal, and she falls asleep very quickly.

The following morning, the pupils get up before light. Bible lessons begin immediately. At breakfast, an hour later, the porridge is found to be burnt and Jane recounts that 'Breakfast was over, and none had breakfasted'. After morning lessons, Miss Temple, Jane's teacher, announces that "a lunch of bread and cheese shall be served to all".

Afterwards, Jane meets Helen Burns. Helen is able to explain to Jane that Lowood "is partly a charity-school: you and I, and all the rest of us, are charity-children".

Later on, Jane sees Helen being punished by Miss Scatcherd.

- The weather in this chapter is cold and miserable, and reflects the harsh way in which the pupils are treated. This is an example of **pathetic fallacy**.
- There is a great deal of emphasis on religion and religious teaching, which seems to be at odds with the way in which the pupils are treated. This suggests that the school is being run in a **hypocritical** way.

---

graven image a carved idol used as an object of worship

hypocritical pretending to be good, moral or honourable but never actually demonstrating these qualities

pathetic fallacy where nature suggests human emotions or sympathies

- Helen is presented as being much more serious than Jane through her choice of reading material.

> **Key quotations**
>
> She looks as if she were thinking of something beyond her punishment— beyond her situation: of something not round her nor before her.

Volume 1, Chapter 6

The next day, it is so cold that they can't wash because the water is frozen. Jane's time as a pupil at Lowood begins, and she sees Helen Burns in a History lesson. It is obvious that Miss Scatcherd is victimizing Helen, and Jane is shocked that she does not defend herself. She is even more shocked when 'the teacher instantly and sharply inflicted on her neck a dozen strokes with [a] bunch of twigs'. This makes Jane angry, but Helen makes no reaction.

In the evening, the weather worsens and this makes Jane feel 'a strange excitement, and reckless and feverish'. As she explores the house, she comes across Helen and they discuss why she does not respond to the punishment. Helen tries to teach Jane the New Testament values, urging her to "Read the New Testament [...] make his word your rule, and his conduct your example". While Jane says that she "must dislike those who [...] persist in disliking me", Helen says that "Life appears to me too short to be spent in nursing animosity, or registering wrongs".

- The conversation between Jane and Helen helps to explain more about Lowood and also emphasizes the difference between the two characters.

> **Key quotations**
>
> "It is far better to endure patiently a smart which nobody feels but yourself, than to commit a hasty action whose evil consequences will extend to all connected with you—and, besides, the Bible bids us return good for evil."

Volume 1, Chapter 7

Time passes and Jane struggles to settle in to life at Lowood. The weather remains cold and what little food there is is stolen from the younger girls by the older ones.

Mr Brocklehurst comes to visit, and immediately criticizes Miss Temple for the way in which she is running the school. He claims that it is Christian to deny the pupils food. He picks on one of the girls who has curly hair, demanding that it should be cut off. When his family arrive, however, Jane notes that one of his daughters has curled hair, showing his hypocrisy.

Mr Brocklehurst recognizes Jane and sets out to humiliate her in front of the school, describing her as a liar and "a little castaway: not a member of the true flock, but evidently an interloper and an alien".

Forced to stand on a stool in front of the school, Jane is able to bear her punishment thanks to Helen's support.

Helen helps Jane during her time at Lowood

> **Key quotations**
>
> "[...] my mission is to mortify in these girls the lusts of the flesh; to teach them to clothe themselves with shame-facedness and sobriety, not with braided hair and costly apparel [...]"

Activity 2

1. Make a list of the things that you learn about life at Lowood School in Chapters 6 and 7. Include evidence from the text to support each of your points.

2. Now look closely at the language that Brontë uses to describe the school and the way in which the children in it are treated. What does this reveal to us about Brontë's attitude to schools such as this?

Volume 1, Chapter 8

Jane is upset by what has happened, and cries. Helen tries to comfort her. Helen's Christian faith is clear once again as she tells Jane that she should think less about what people think of her.

Miss Temple invites both girls to her rooms and asks Jane to tell her what happened. Jane does, keeping in mind 'Helen's warnings against the indulgence of resentment'. Miss Temple and Helen talk in front of the fire and the girls then return to the bedroom where Helen is once again told off by Miss Scatcherd.

As the chapter closes, Miss Temple reveals to the school that Jane is innocent and Jane begins to enjoy her time at Lowood.

- Miss Temple is once again shown to be a good Christian woman who cares about her pupils.

- Jane's more measured approach to telling her story suggests that Helen's advice and good nature are beginning to have a positive impact on her.

- Helen's illness and death are **foreshadowed** in this chapter with Miss Temple's 'sad sigh' on seeing her leave the room.

I had meant to be so good, and to do so much at Lowood; to make so many friends, to earn respect, and win affection.

"[…] if others don't love me, I would rather die than live—I cannot bear to be solitary and hated, Helen."

"[…] you think too much of the love of human beings […]"

I would not now have exchanged Lowood with all its privations, for Gateshead and its daily luxuries.

Volume 1, Chapter 9

As the weather improves, Jane enjoys exploring the countryside. However, there is a dark side to this freedom. Typhus, a deadly disease, has infected Lowood and many of the students are dead or dying.

Jane describes a new friendship that she has made, and reveals that this has come about because Helen is sick. She only realizes when she sees the surgeon that Helen's illness is very serious.

Late that night, Jane creeps up to Miss Temple's room, where Helen is sleeping, to 'give her one last kiss, exchange with her one last word'. She and Helen talk about their attitudes to death and Helen reveals that she is relieved to die young.

Jane holds Helen as she falls asleep. When she awakes, she is being carried back to her own bed. Helen has died.

- Jane addresses the reader directly in this chapter. This is used to heighten the tension.
- It is clear that Jane is growing up. She begins to think about the nature of life and death, heaven and hell for the first time.
- The passages concerning Helen's death are full of **pathos**.

"By dying young I shall escape great sufferings."

foreshadowed hinted at

pathos a quality that causes the reader to feel sympathy and sadness

Activity 3

Look again at the passage which begins **"You came to bid me good-bye, then"** and ends **'inscribed with her name, and the word "Resurgam"'**.

- How does Brontë create pathos in this passage? Look at the language that is used to describe the speech and actions of the characters, and also at what they say and do.
- What lessons does Helen try to teach Jane in this passage?

Volume 1, Chapter 10

The typhus outbreak draws attention to Lowood and changes are made to the school. Jane remains there for another eight years, first as a pupil and then as a teacher.

Miss Temple leaves and Jane is reminded that there is a world outside of Lowood. She advertises for a position as a **governess** and is offered one at Thornfield Hall, where she will work for Mrs Fairfax. As she is about to leave Lowood, a visitor arrives. It is Bessie, the Reed family maid, with news of the Reeds and also of Jane's uncle who called at Gateshead looking for her several years earlier.

- The opening paragraph reminds us that this is a retrospective narrative, with the adult Jane telling us that she will 'pass a space of eight years almost in silence'.
- Jane's increased maturity is reflected in her decisiveness.
- Bessie's description of the fates of the Reed children suggests that Jane, despite her difficult circumstances, has fared better than they have.

> **Key quotations**
>
> [...] the real world was wide, and that a varied field of hopes and fears, of sensations and excitements, awaited those who had courage to go forth into its expanse to seek real knowledge of life amidst its perils.
>
> I desired liberty; for liberty I gasped; for liberty I uttered a prayer.

Volume 1, Chapter 11

Jane travels to Thornfield Hall. She is anxious about the change that she is making, and tells the reader that 'It is a very strange sensation to inexperienced youth to feel itself quite alone in the world'.

Eventually, she arrives at Thornfield Hall where she is greeted by Mrs Fairfax, the housekeeper, who immediately puts her at ease.

The following day, she meets her **ward**, Adèle Varens, for the first time. Adèle tells Jane some of how she came to be at Thornfield, and about Mr Rochester, the owner of the estate. Jane is also told more by Mrs Fairfax, although she is unable to answer Jane's questions.

Jane is given a tour of the house, and meets Grace Poole, a seamstress and housemaid, for the first time.

- Jane is now established as an educated woman, yet she retains her fascination with stories and has a vivid imagination.
- The reference to 'Bluebeard's castle' foreshadows the discovery of the madwoman in the attic later in the novel.

> **Key quotations**
>
> "I anticipated only coldness and stiffness: this is not like what I have heard of the treatment of governesses; but I must not exult too soon."
>
> [...] the last sound I expected to hear in so still a region, a laugh, struck my ear. It was a curious laugh; distinct, formal, mirthless.

Activity 4

Look again at the passage which begins 'It was a fine Autumn morning' and ends 'its old tower-top looked over a knoll between the house and gates'.

Using the description as a guide, draw a picture of Thornfield Hall as Jane sees it. Label it with quotations from the text.

Volume 1, Chapter 12

After three months at Thornfield, Jane is rather bored: 'restlessness was in my nature'. She occupies herself, when she is not teaching, with long walks or climbing to the attic and daydreaming.

One day, she walks to Hay to post a letter, and stops to watch the sunset. While she is there, she is interrupted by a dog, a horse and his rider. The horse slips on the ice, and the rider falls off. Jane helps him back onto his horse, noting that she 'felt no fear of him, and but little shyness'. They talk briefly, and she reveals that she lives at Thornfield. As he rides off, Jane thinks about the incident, and reiterates that she is no longer happy to have a simply passive existence.

When she returns to Thornfield, she sees the dog that she saw earlier, and Mrs Fairfax tells her that the dog belongs to the master of the house, Mr Rochester.

> **governess** a woman employed by a wealthy family to educate their children in their own home
>
> **ward** the child that she is responsible for

- Rochester's comment that "necessity compels me to make you useful" foreshadows his later reliance on Jane.
- Her increasing dissatisfaction with her position in life suggests that she is moving away from the conventional path that Lowood prepared her for.

> **Key quotations**
>
> It is in vain to say human beings ought to be satisfied with tranquillity: they must have action; and they will make it if they cannot find it.
>
> Women are supposed to be very calm generally: but women feel just as men feel.

> **Activity 5**
>
> Re-read the first part of Chapter 12, up to 'It is thoughtless to condemn them, or laugh at them, if they seek to do more or learn more than custom has pronounced necessary for their sex'. In this section, Jane shows that she is unhappy with the life that she is expected to lead.
>
> Copy and complete the table below to identify examples of her unhappiness and what these suggest to the reader.
>
> | Quotation | What this suggests to the reader |
> | --- | --- |
> | 'I longed for a power of vision [...] which might reach the busy world' | She wants to experience a busier life than she experiences in the countryside. |
> | | |

Volume 1, Chapter 13

The atmosphere at Thornfield is much livelier now that Rochester has arrived. Jane and Adèle are invited to have tea with him, and he takes the opportunity to find out more about her.

Rochester compliments Jane's teaching of Adèle and asks her about her time at Lowood. He looks at some of her paintings and seems very interested in them, but then abruptly suggests that 'he was tired of our company, and wished to dismiss us'. Mrs Fairfax explains that Rochester has some troubles in his life, but does not explain more fully.

- Rochester asks Jane about her family, and she is not entirely truthful with him, telling him that she has "none that I ever saw". He therefore thinks that she has no relatives to interfere when he later asks her to marry him.
- Her paintings suggest that she is wild and unconventional.
- Jane's descriptions of Rochester suggest that he is a **Byronic hero**: mad, bad and dangerous to know.

Key quotations

"When you came on me in Hay Lane last night, I thought unaccountably of fairy tales, and had half a mind to demand whether you had bewitched my horse."

Volume 1, Chapter 14

For several days, Jane does not see anything of Rochester. Then she and Adèle are called to see him. Rochester gives Adèle a gift box and sends her to play with it so that he can talk to Jane undisturbed. She describes how he is 'in his after-dinner mood' and they talk freely. Jane comments that she should have been 'conventionally vague and polite' in response to his questions, but she speaks honestly to him as if she were his equal.

When he suggests that he has "a right to be a little masterful", she holds her own in the debate. It is clear that his respect for her grows during this chapter as he listens to her advice. He shows his understanding of her character when he reflects that "The Lowood constraint still clings to you" and suggests that he wishes to see more of the "vivid, restless, resolute captive".

At the end of the chapter, he reflects on his relationship with Adèle's mother.

- Jane's comment that 'There was a smile on his lips, and his eyes sparkled' suggests to the reader that he has fallen for her. She, however, naïvely believes that it is because he has drunk too much wine. This reminds us that a book written only in the **first person** cannot always be relied on to be wholly accurate in its presentation of events – Jane can occasionally be an **unreliable narrator**.
- Rochester reveals more about the troubles that Mrs Fairfax **alluded to** in the previous chapter, and admits that he feels remorse for them.
- Jane's advice to Rochester indicates that she has grown up considerably. The impulsive and emotional Jane Eyre who arrived at Lowood has been replaced by a more reflective young woman.

Key quotations

"[...] do you agree with me that I have a right to be a little masterful, abrupt; perhaps exacting, sometimes [...]"

"When fate wronged me, I had not the wisdom to remain cool: I turned desperate; then I degenerated."

allude to refer to something indirectly

Byronic hero a type of male character created by Lord Byron who is typically brooding, rebellious and darkly romantic

first person a story written from the viewpoint of a character writing or speaking directly about themselves using 'I'

unreliable narrator a first-person narrator who sometimes fails to tell the truth or recount events accurately, allowing a reader to draw their own conclusions

Volume 1, Chapter 15

Rochester tells Jane about his doomed love affair with Adèle's mother, Céline. He also reflects upon the nature of love, but comments that Jane has yet to experience it: **"your soul sleeps; the shock is yet to be given which shall waken it"**.

Later, Jane thinks about her relationship with Rochester. She has developed 'a keen **delight in receiving the new ideas he offered'** and looks forward to his company.

That night, she is awakened by a strange noise and hears **'a demoniac laugh'**. Finding smoke in the corridor, she follows it to its source and finds that Rochester's bed, with him in it, is on fire. Jane is able to put the fire out, and he awakens. He tells her to tell no one about what has happened. Meanwhile, he goes to the third floor.

At the end of the chapter, Rochester thanks her for saving his life, but does not tell her what he has found upstairs. He calls her his **"cherished preserver"**.

- Much of the chapter focuses on Jane's thoughts about Rochester. In this way, she reveals a great deal about her growing affection for him.
- The fire foreshadows the later fire which destroys the house.

Volume 2, Chapter 1

When Jane finds Rochester the next morning, he and Grace Poole are restoring the room to order. Jane asks Grace what happened. Grace, in return, questions Jane about what she might have heard, and warns her that **"it is as well to have a drawn bolt between one and any mischief that may be about"**.

Jane decides that Grace must harbour desire for Rochester and has set the fire. This leads to her thinking about her own relationship with him, and she reveals that she thinks that **"perhaps Mr. Rochester approves [her]: at any rate you have often felt as if he did"**.

Rochester leaves to attend a party. In conversation with Mrs Fairfax, Jane learns that he is **"a general favourite"** with society ladies and with the beautiful Blanche Ingram in particular. Jane realizes that she has been foolish: **"It does good to no woman to be flattered by her superior, who cannot possibly intend to marry her"**.

- Grace's warning to Jane to lock her door foreshadows later events.

Tips for assessment

Upgrade

In your assessment, you will need to show off your knowledge of the text, but this will not be enough to get you a high mark. As well as knowing *what* happens, you will also need to be able to write about:

- how events are linked
- what events reveal about the characters
- why Brontë chose to present certain events in the way that she did.

Volume 2, Chapter 2

Ten days pass and Rochester still does not return. When Mrs Fairfax receives a letter from him, Jane is excited by the fact that he will be back in three days. As the household prepares for his return, and the arrival of his guests, Jane overhears some of the servants talking and realizes that 'there was a mystery at Thornfield; and that from participation in that mystery, I was purposely excluded'.

When the party arrives, Jane and Adèle watch from a distance. The following day, they are summoned to the drawing room. Jane sits in the window seat with a book, and observes the guests as they come into the room. She acknowledges their presence with a curtsey, and although some of them acknowledge her, 'the others only stared at me'.

She describes each of the guests in turn, commenting of Blanche Ingram that 'Genius is said to be self-conscious: I cannot tell whether Miss Ingram was a genius, but she was self-conscious—remarkably self-conscious indeed'.

Jane overhears Blanche speaking negatively about governesses and directly criticizing her. Rochester encourages Blanche in this. While the guests play music and sing, Jane quietly leaves. Rochester follows her and insists that she comes to join the party every evening.

At the very end of the chapter, it is clear that Rochester has strong feelings for Jane: "Good night, my——".

- When the letter from Rochester is opened, Jane proves that she is an unreliable narrator as she attributes her reaction to the fact that 'it was hot, and I attributed to that circumstance a fiery glow which suddenly rose to my face'.
- The passage about governesses reminds the reader of Jane's position within the house, and society as a whole.

> **Key quotations**
>
> "He is not of your order: keep to your caste; and be too self-respecting to lavish the love of the whole heart, soul, and strength, where such a gift is not wanted and would be despised."

Volume 2, Chapter 3

Jane describes how the atmosphere at Thornfield Hall has changed: 'All sad feelings seemed now driven from the house, all gloomy associations forgotten'. The house is busy and full.

Jane uses the opportunity to observe Blanche Ingram and to note that 'he was going to marry her, for family, perhaps political reasons; because her rank and connexions suited him'. She also realizes that Rochester is watching her 'closely, keenly, shrewdly'. Although she claims not to be jealous, she is judgemental of Blanche: 'her pride and self-complacency repelled further and further what she wished to allure'.

In the evening, Richard Mason arrives unexpectedly while Rochester is absent. Jane describes him as 'unsettled and inanimate' but the other guests are very taken with him.

A gipsy arrives and insists upon telling the ladies' fortunes. Blanche, in particular, is very keen to have her fortune told. Then Jane is summoned by the gipsy. She reveals that she is excited by the opportunity.

Rochester torments Jane with his courtship of Blanche Ingram

- The game of charades foreshadows the events of the following chapter.

- Disguise is a key element of this chapter, with dramatic entrances and exits heightening the drama of the events.

- Throughout the chapter, Rochester flirts with Miss Ingram seemingly with the intention of making Jane feel jealous.

- Jane's views on marriage are clearly at odds with those of the men and women of Rochester's class, who are motivated by the 'commonplace' motives of 'interest and connexions'. She, however, believes in marriages based on love.

Volume 2, Chapter 4

The gipsy seems intent on asking Jane questions, and Jane becomes suspicious. The conversation becomes more intimate and reveals details about Rochester's 'fortune' as well as her own. Jane is surprised at how much the gipsy knows of her.

When Rochester finally reveals himself as 'the gipsy', Jane tells him that she believes "you have been trying to draw me out—or in".

Jane reveals that Mason has arrived, and Rochester is shocked. She tells Rochester that she would give her "life to serve" him. At the end of the chapter, Jane hears Rochester show Mason to his room.

- The references to the fire and how it scorches her is suggestive of the passion that Rochester kindles in Jane. She recognizes the danger, but is powerless to do anything to stop it.

- Rochester's shock at the arrival of Mason and his reliance on Jane for support remind us of how she helped him when he fell from his horse, and also foreshadow future events.

Volume 2, Chapter 5

Jane is woken in the night by the moonlight and, as she goes to shut the curtain, 'The night—its silence—its rest, was rent in twain by a savage, a sharp, a shrilly sound that ran from end to end of Thornfield Hall'. She hears 'a struggle: a deadly one' taking place overhead and, when she steps outside her room, she sees that the guests have also been awoken. Rochester appears and tells them that a servant has had a nightmare. Jane returns to her room and waits for him to come for her.

When he does so, he takes her up to the floor above, where Mason is bleeding. Rochester tells Jane to take care of Mason but that she must not speak to him. When Rochester leaves, Jane considers the mysteries that the house holds.

Later Rochester brings with him a doctor who examines Mason and finds that he has been both bitten and stabbed. Mason declares that "She sucked the blood: she said she'd drain my heart", which Rochester treats dismissively, although Jane sees him 'shudder' when he hears it.

Having been treated for his injuries, Mason leaves. Discussing the events of the night, Rochester refers to Jane as his "pet lamb".

Rochester hints about his past as a "wild boy" and suggests that he may be able to **redeem** his past actions through a "genial stranger". Suddenly changing the subject, he turns it to his possible marriage to Blanche.

- The blood sucking reference links Bertha to a vampire, and the fact that this event takes place under a full moon reinforces this view of her as something other-worldly and dangerous.
- Rochester's comments about having "warned" Mason and his remark that "I have striven long to avoid exposure, and I should not like it to come at last" indicate an expectation that something terrible might happen and foreshadow future events.
- The description of the nature and beauty of the garden contrasts with that of the house, and presents the setting as **Edenic**.

> **Key quotations**
>
> What crime was this, that lived incarnate in this sequestered mansion, and could neither be expelled nor subdued by the owner?
>
> "This wound was not done with a knife: there have been teeth here!"

Edenic a paradise, like the biblical Garden of Eden

redeem save from the consequences of sin, or make up for faults

Volume 2, Chapter 6

Jane recalls a memory from her childhood when she heard that 'to dream of children was a sure sign of trouble, either to one's self or one's kin', and reveals that she has been dreaming of 'an infant'. The next day, she is visited by Mrs Reed's former coachman who has come to tell her that the Reeds are in "great trouble". John has died and Mrs Reed has had a stroke. She has sent for Jane.

Jane tells Rochester she wants to visit her aunt. He is surprised and suggests that she shouldn't go. When Jane insists, he is keen that she only goes for a week. He gives her money to take with her, and she tells him that Adèle should go to school when he marries. He tells her not to advertise for a new position and to "trust this quest of a situation to [him]".

Jane arrives at Gateshead where Mrs Reed is still alive. When Jane enters, she is reminded of the difficult times that she had at Gateshead. Georgiana and Eliza are both there and are polite to her, although Jane notes that 'Young ladies have a remarkable way of letting you know that they think you a "quiz," without actually saying the words'. Jane is surprised by how little she now cares about their treatment of her, and insists (against their wishes) that they tell Mrs Reed that she has arrived.

When Jane sees Mrs Reed, she shows great compassion to her but Mrs Reed 'turn[s] her face rather from [Jane]'. It is clear that Mrs Reed has not forgotten her dislike of Jane.

In the ten days until Jane next sees her, she spends the time drawing. Georgiana and Eliza see her drawing of Rochester. She walks in the grounds with Georgiana several times. Eliza, however, spends her time alone. Eventually Eliza reveals that John's behaviour 'had been a source of profound affliction to her' but that she has now made plans for the future – which do not include Georgiana.

One day, Mrs Reed reveals to Jane a letter sent to Mrs Reed three years previously by Jane's uncle, John Eyre. In the letter, Jane's uncle expresses a wish to adopt Jane and **bequeath** his **estate** to her. Mrs Reed did not pass on the letter because she "disliked [Jane] too fixedly and thoroughly ever to lend a hand in lifting [her] to prosperity". Jane tells her not to think about it any further, but Mrs Reed then reveals that she wrote and told John Eyre that Jane had died.

Jane tells her aunt that she "long[s] earnestly to be reconciled" but Mrs Reed 'shrank from [her] touch'. Jane tells her that she forgives her and, later that day, Mrs Reed dies.

---

bequeath to leave someone something when you die

estate a person's assets, for example their property and money

Activity 6

Copy and complete the table below to show how Brontë's presentation of the Reed family changes throughout the story. Explain what this suggests about the changing attitudes of characters in the novel and include quotations from the text to support your ideas.

	Presentation of the character in the early part of the novel	Presentation of the character in Volume 2, Chapter 6	How does the character change? What does this suggest?
Eliza Reed			
Georgiana Reed		Eliza: "Georgiana, a more vain and absurd animal than you, was certainly never allowed to cumber the earth."	
John Reed	Jane calls John "a tyrant".	Mrs Reed: "John is sunk and degraded—his look is frightful—I feel ashamed for him when I see him."	
Mrs Reed		Jane: "Poor, suffering woman!"	Jane has matured and is able to see past her dislike of her aunt.

Volume 2, Chapter 7

It is another month before Jane is ready to return to Thornfield Hall. When Jane returns, she tells no one of her plans. She thinks about her relationship with Adèle and Rochester, and meets him unexpectedly on a path near the house. She is pleased to see him, and it seems that he is also pleased to see her. They discuss his upcoming wedding, with him saying **"I wish, Jane, I were a trifle better adapted to match with her externally"**. As he allows her past him on the path, she tells him that **"wherever you are is my home,—my only home"**.

At the house, everyone is pleased to see her and Jane notes that **'there is no happiness like that of being loved by your fellow-creatures'**.

A fortnight passes, and there seem to be no wedding plans. Jane begins to hope that **'the match was broken off'**.

Key quotations

But what is so headstrong as youth? What so blind as inexperience?

Volume 2, Chapter 8

It is Midsummer's Eve, and Jane is walking in the garden when she meets Rochester without warning. He asks her to walk with him and although she 'did not like to walk at this hour alone with Mr. Rochester in the shadowy orchard', she does so. They discuss the impending marriage again, and he reveals that he will be married in a month. Rochester talks of his feelings for Jane: "it is as if I had a string somewhere under my left ribs, tightly and inextricably knotted to a similar string situated in the corresponding quarter of your little frame".

Jane reveals the depth of her feelings for him, and he kisses her. As she gets up to leave, he asks her to marry him. Jane questions his sincerity and, after much discussion, she agrees.

As the storm breaks around the house, Jane joyfully returns to her room. In the morning, Adèle reveals that the tree that they had sat under the night before has been 'struck by lightning in the night, and half of it split away'.

- Rochester's possessive language when he describes Jane as "my little wife" and says that "I must have you for my own" likens Jane to a possession and foreshadows her later concern about her position.
- Rochester defies both God and man by asking Jane to marry him, and is punished by the lightning.
- The pathetic fallacy of the storm links to the idea that their relationship defies nature.

Volume 2, Chapter 9

The following morning, Jane wonders whether the proposal was a dream. She fears that her appearance has changed because of her 'blissful [...] mood'.

Mrs Fairfax breakfasts with Jane but is quiet. When Jane sees Rochester, he reveals that they will be married in just four weeks. He talks of his plans for the wedding but Jane's ideas and his are very different. He wants her to wear jewels and satin, but she feels that this would make her "an ape in a harlequin's jacket,—a jay in borrowed plumes".

Rochester tells Mrs Fairfax the news alone, and when Jane sees her, she is shocked by her reaction. Mrs Fairfax questions Rochester's reason for marrying her and suggests that Jane should "keep Mr. Rochester at a distance: [...] Gentlemen in his station are not accustomed to marry their governesses".

In Millcote, Jane 'hated the business' of trying on dresses and visiting the jeweller's shop. She 'burned with a sense of annoyance and degradation' at her dependence on Rochester and resolves to ask her uncle for a "small [...] independency".

When they return to Thornfield Hall, Jane tries to assert her independence by refusing to spend all her time with Rochester. That evening, he sings to her about how much he loves her, but she keeps him at a distance, telling him that 'he should know fully what sort of a bargain he had made'.

Over the course of the next month, she maintains her distance and 'Mrs. Fairfax, I saw approved me: her anxiety on my account vanished'.

- Rochester tells Adèle that "mademoiselle shall live with me [...] and only me". This again shows his possessive side.
- It is **ironic** that his actions in treating Jane as a possession are the cause of her writing to her uncle, since this is how his intended **bigamy** is revealed.

Volume 2, Chapter 10

On the evening of the wedding, Jane 'had at heart a strange and anxious thought'. Rochester has been called away on business.

Later, she tells him that she has been thinking about the wedding and their life together, and her dream in which she was walking through the ruins of Thornfield Hall carrying a child. She also reveals that when she woke she saw a woman with "a savage face" in her room, wearing her wedding veil. Rochester assures her that she was "The creature of an over-stimulated brain" and that, once they are married, "there shall be no recurrence of these mental terrors".

When shown the torn veil, he says that it must have been Grace Poole in her room, and tells her to sleep with Adèle that night, and to lock the door. That night, Jane does not sleep.

- The narrative of this chapter is not **chronological**, so the reader does not find out about the night's events until Rochester does.
- Rochester's determination to take Jane away from Thornfield Hall is made clear: he says that "we shall leave Thornfield to-morrow, within half an hour after our return from church".
- Jane's concerns about her new life are also revealed when she refers to her marriage as "*your* [Rochester's] life" and to herself as 'Jane Rochester, a person whom as yet I knew not'.
- It is ironic that Jane refers to 'Mrs. Rochester! She did not exist' when she has, in fact, been visited by her in the night.

> **Key quotations**
>
> "I thought of the life that lay before me—*your* life, sir—an existence more expansive and stirring than my own [...]"
>
> "I dreamt another dream, sir: that Thornfield Hall was a dreary ruin, the retreat of bats and owls."

bigamy being married to more than one person at the same time

chronological arranged in the order of time in which events occurred

irony words that express the opposite of what is meant

Rochester's bigamy is revealed at the altar

Volume 2, Chapter 11

Rochester's impatience is revealed when he 'sent up to ask why I did not come' on the morning of the wedding. Jane does not recognize herself in the mirror wearing the bridal clothes. Jane notes that Rochester is 'bent up to a purpose, so grimly resolute', which seems unusual on his wedding day.

Jane notices strangers in the churchyard and assumes that they will come in to watch the service. Just as they are about to be married, the service is interrupted by one of the strangers who claims that there is a reason they cannot be married. Rochester's reaction is simply to hold Jane closer to him as the stranger reveals that Rochester is already married.

The second stranger turns out to be Mason, and he tells the **clergyman** that Rochester's wife lives at Thornfield Hall. At this, Rochester mutters "I took care that none should hear of it" before admitting to everyone that "the mysterious lunatic [...] is my wife".

Rochester and Jane leave the church and he takes her to the room at the top of the house where 'a figure ran backwards and forwards' and then attacks Rochester. As Jane and the solicitor leave, he reveals that it was her uncle who uncovered the truth of Rochester's intended bigamy thanks to Jane's letter.

Jane locks herself in her room, feeling that she is 'a cold, solitary girl again' and that her 'faith was blighted—confidence destroyed!' In her despair, she turns to God.

- Jane refers to herself in the **third person** at the end of the chapter, perhaps suggesting that she feels emotionally distant from the situation.
- After Bertha attacks Rochester, she is tied to a chair. This is reminiscent of Jane's punishment in the red room and suggests that both characters are similarly oppressed.

clergyman a priest or vicar in the Christian Church

incarcerated imprisoned

third person from the perspective of a character or voice outside the story, using the pronouns 'he' or 'she'

In the deep shade, at the further end of the room, a figure ran backwards and forwards. What it was, whether beast or human being, one could not, at first sight, tell: it grovelled, seemingly, on all fours; it snatched and growled like some strange wild animal: but it was covered with clothing; and a quantity of dark, grizzled hair, wild as a mane, hid its head and face.

Volume 3, Chapter 1

Jane decides that she must leave Thornfield. Even though she does not really want to leave Rochester, she feels that she 'should do it'. She realizes that no one has been to see her since she locked herself in her room. When she attempts to leave the room, she falls over Rochester who was sitting guard at her door. He tells her that he has waited there for all the time that she has been inside and he asks for her forgiveness. He tries to comfort her, but she rejects him.

Rochester says that he will "nail up the front door" of Thornfield Hall to keep Bertha **incarcerated**. He tells Jane that they will leave the following day but she will not agree to go with him: "I must part with you for my whole life". He tries to convince her to go with him to France but Jane will not consent to be his "mistress".

In desperation, Rochester explains that he met Bertha in Jamaica and that he barely knew her before they were married. Once it was discovered that she was mad, it was too late for him to escape the marriage. He tells her that he once considered committing suicide, but decided instead to return to Europe where he could "See that she [was] cared for as her condition demands". He explains how she came to be locked in the attic at Thornfield Hall, and how she has frequently escaped, including appearing in Jane's room and wearing her wedding veil.

Despite his marriage to Bertha, he claims that he thought it "absolutely rational that I should be considered free to love and be loved". He talks of his relationships with his mistresses as being "a grovelling fashion of existence", and Jane realizes that, were she to become his mistress, 'he would one day regard [her] with the same feeling which now in his mind desecrated their memory'.

Rochester tells Jane that when he met her, he "found what I can truly love". Despite his feelings, Jane knows that her 'intolerable duty' is to leave. She tells him to "trust in God and yourself" but Rochester believes that his actions "transgress a mere human law" and have hurt no one.

Jane leaves the following day.

- References to "pluck out your right eye [...] cut off your right hand" are biblical and, in this case, relate to the idea that Jane has offended God by her actions and must be punished.
- Jane reveals the depth of her humanity when she tells Rochester that Bertha "cannot help being mad".

- Rochester refers to the "antipodes of the Creole", which suggests that Bertha is mixed race.
- Jane's religion and morality are clearly evident in this chapter. She refers to the fact that "Laws and principles are not for the times when there is no temptation".
- The reader is directly addressed, drawing attention to the retrospective nature of the narrative.

> **Key quotations**
>
> Reader!—I forgave him at the moment, and on the spot.
>
> "Bertha Mason,—the true daughter of an infamous mother,—dragged me through all the hideous and degrading agonies which must attend a man bound to a wife at once intemperate and unchaste."

Volume 3, Chapter 2

Two days later, Jane has arrived at Whitcross having spent all of her money to get there. She is 'absolutely destitute'. Exhausted and hungry, she walks on the heath feeling God's presence and praying that he will take care of Rochester.

Eventually, she arrives in a village where she attempts to find work but is rejected several times. Finally, she manages to beg some bread and porridge and wanders near the village in the darkness. Suddenly, she sees a light and is drawn to it. Arriving at the building, she looks through the window and sees two women and a servant. Hannah, the servant, tells Jane that "we can't take in a vagrant to lodge" and Jane feels 'A pang of exquisite suffering'.

Jane is saved by the arrival of St. John Rivers who takes her into Moor House. At the end of the chapter, Jane 'thanked God [...] and slept'.

- The light in the window suggests the light of God, and offers her hope for the future.
- Jane's faith now reflects that of Helen Burns—she believes that God will protect both her and Rochester.

> **Key quotations**
>
> Somehow, now that I had once crossed the threshold of this house, and once was brought face to face with its owners, I felt no longer outcast, vagrant, and disowned by the wide world.

Volume 3, Chapter 3

Three days and nights pass with Jane lying ill in bed, looked after by Hannah, Diana and Mary. She notes that 'Never once in their dialogues did I hear a syllable of regret at the hospitality they had extended to me'. As she recovers, she becomes involved in the life of the family and learns more about St. John Rivers.

Jane tells them that she is "completely isolated from every connection" and tells the family only as much of her story "as [she] can tell without compromising [her] own peace of mind". She does not even tell them her real name, but admits that this is the case, telling them that she fears discovery.

St. John agrees to help her.

> **Key quotations**
>
> Prejudices, it is well known, are most difficult to eradicate from the heart whose soil has never been loosened or fertilized by education: they grow there, firm as weeds among stones.

Volume 3, Chapter 4

Jane states that 'The more I knew of the inmates of Moor House, the better I liked them' and she discovers that they have a great deal in common.

Her relationship with Diana and Mary is described in detail, showing the depth of her feelings for them, but she is clear that her relationship with St. John is more distant, in part because he is rarely there.

When she hears St. John preach, she sees a very different side to him: 'The heart was thrilled, the mind astonished, by the power of the preacher' but she notes that he 'had not yet found that peace of God which passeth all understanding'.

Diana and Mary are due to leave to become governesses, and St. John finds Jane a position as the **mistress** of a school in Morton. Jane accepts the position.

He tells her that he thinks that she will not stay long because "human affections and sympathies have a most powerful hold on you" and reveals that he is not really content in his work.

At the end of the chapter, it is revealed that the Rivers' uncle John has died and has left them just thirty guineas. The rest of his fortune has been left to another relation. The next day, Jane leaves to take up her new position.

> **Activity 7**
>
> Jane's experience of life at Moor House is positive, and she tells us that 'There was a reviving pleasure in this intercourse, of a kind now tasted by me for the first time—the pleasure arising from perfect congeniality of tastes, sentiments, and principles'.
>
> Her relationships with Diana, Mary and St. John Rivers are a significant element of this. Find quotations from the novel that show how Jane feels about each member of the Rivers family. What do these quotations suggest about her relationship with the Rivers family?

mistress teacher

Volume 3, Chapter 5

Jane describes the cottage that is now her home and her new life. She says that she does not expect to find happiness because she is 'weakly dismayed at the ignorance, the poverty, the coarseness of all [she] heard and saw round [her]'.

She reflects on her decision to leave Thornfield, and on the fact that Rochester 'did love me—no one will ever love me so again'.

When St. John comes to visit her, he is concerned about her. He advises her "to resist, firmly, every temptation which would incline you to look back". He reveals that he "burnt for the more active life of the world" but that he has resolved to be a **missionary** and will shortly leave for the East.

As they talk, a woman, Rosamond Oliver, approaches them. Jane describes her as an 'earthly angel'. Jane notes St. John's 'solemn eye melt with sudden fire, and flicker with resistless emotion'. It is clear that St. John and Rosamond are mutually attracted but they seem to be unable to do anything about it.

> **Key quotations**
>
> I must not forget that these coarsely-clad little peasants are of flesh and blood as good as the scions of gentlest genealogy; and that the germs of native excellence, refinement, intelligence, kind feeling, are as likely to exist in their hearts as in those of the best-born.
>
> God has given us, in a measure, the power to make our own fate.

Volume 3, Chapter 6

Over time, Jane finds more pleasure in her work at the school. She becomes friendly with Rosamond Oliver.

Jane is drawing a miniature of Rosamond when St. John comes to visit her. He admires it and she offers him a version of it for when he goes to be a missionary. His reply "That I should like to have it, is certain: whether it would be judicious or wise is another question" suggests that he is concerned about his feelings for Rosamond. Jane tells him that he should take the drawing and they spend time discussing his relationship with Rosamond. However, he reveals that he thinks that Rosamond "would not make me a good wife".

St. John is shocked by Jane's response: 'He had not imagined that a woman would dare to speak [as she does] to a man' but eventually tells her that he does not want a copy of the painting. As she leaves, he tears 'a narrow slip from the margin' from her paper.

missionary member of a religious group that spreads the teachings of that religion in another country

Volume 3, Chapter 7

The following day, St. John returns and Jane 'began to feel his wits were touched' as a result of his strange behaviour and his impatience "to hear the sequel" to a story that he has only heard part of. He reveals that he now knows that she is Jane Eyre thanks to the slip of paper which he tore from the painting.

He reveals that her uncle John is dead and that she is "quite an heiress". She is taken aback by the news. He also reveals that the Rivers are her cousins. She is more pleased by this news than the news of her fortune, and decides that she will divide her fortune between them all.

They discuss Jane's marriage prospects and she states that she will never marry. He advises her she should not be so sure of this, but she replies "I know what I feel, and how averse are my inclinations to the bare thought of marriage".

- Jane is revealed as the unknown relative mentioned in Volume 3, Chapter 4.
- The independence which she sought during Volume 2, Chapter 9 is now finally hers. Since she is unmarried, she can decide for herself how to spend her fortune.
- The details of the story are revealed slowly, enabling the reader to experience Jane's pleasure at finding a family at last.

Activity 8

Jane comments that "No one would take me for love; and I will not be regarded in the light of a mere money-speculation". What does this quotation:

- reveal about the attitudes of the day towards women?
- reveal about the character of Jane?
- suggest about Brontë's own view of such attitudes?

Give reasons for your answers.

Key quotations

One does not jump, and spring, and shout hurrah! at hearing one has got a fortune; one begins to consider responsibilities, and to ponder business [...]

It was a grand boon doubtless; and independence would be glorious [...]

Volume 3, Chapter 8

Now that she is independently wealthy, Jane has given up the school and is readying Moor House for the arrival of Diana and Mary. St. John believes, however, that there are more important things that she should be doing than "common place home pleasures".

The more time she spends with St. John, the more she comes to understand him and she 'comprehended all at once that he would hardly make a good husband: that it would be a trying thing to be his wife' because he is more suited to 'scenes of strife and danger' than anything else. When he has an 'act of duty' to perform is when he is truly happy.

Jane notes that their relationship has changed since they discovered that they are related, and that St. John is now more distant than before.

Jane refuses St. John's proposal of marriage

The family settle back into life together, and St. John persuades her to learn **Hindostanee** rather than German. Eventually, St. John reveals to her his true intentions: he wants Jane to come to India with him. He attempts to overcome all of her reservations about the idea, telling her that she is "docile, diligent, disinterested, faithful, constant, and courageous; very gentle, and very heroic". Eventually, she agrees to go with him, but only if she can "go free". He will not accept this and insists that they must be married. Jane refuses his offer.

- Writing retrospectively, Jane reveals that her life has since changed further as she has 'seen **paysannes** [...] and the best of them seemed to me ignorant, coarse, and besotted, compared with my Morton girls'.

- She does not forget Rochester during this period, and refers to his memory as 'a name graven on a tablet, fated to last as long as the marble it inscribed'.

- Jane is torn between what she sees as "the most glorious [role] man can adopt or God assign" and the fact that if she "join[s] St. John, I abandon half myself: if I go to India, I go to premature death".

- St. John's reference to wanting "a wife: the sole helpmeet I can influence efficiently in life, and retain absolutely till death" reflects Rochester's earlier desire to possess her and suggests that, as a woman, she is unlikely ever to achieve independence in marriage.

- Jane's position at the end of the novel is foreshadowed by St. John's comment about "barren obscurity".

Hindostanee the language of North India and Pakistan

paysannes French peasant women

Volume 3, Chapter 9

St. John remains for an extra week and Jane is made to 'feel what severe punishment a good, yet stern, a conscientious, yet implacable man can inflict on one who has offended him'. She tries to rekindle their friendship but he refuses to accept it, and insists that if she is to come to India with him, it must be as his wife.

Diana and Jane discuss his proposal and Jane notes that "He is a good and a great man: but he forgets, pitilessly, the feelings and claims of little people, in pursuing his own large views".

As she asks for God's guidance, she hears 'the voice of a human being—a known, loved, well-remembered voice—that of Edward Fairfax Rochester [which] spoke in pain and woe wildly, eerily, urgently'. She goes to her room and prays.

Key quotations

To have yielded then would have been an error of principle; to have yielded now would have been an error of judgment.

It was *my* time to assume ascendancy. *My* powers were in play, and in force.

Volume 3, Chapter 10

At dawn, Jane prepares to leave. She recalls her feelings on hearing the voice which 'had opened the doors of the soul's cell, and loosed its bands'. She tells the sisters that she will be going on a journey and sets off 'like the messenger-pigeon flying home'.

When she eventually arrives at Thornfield, she 'looked with timorous joy towards a stately house: I saw a blackened ruin' and she realizes why no one has replied to her letters. She fears that Rochester is dead.

She meets Rochester's former butler who gradually reveals to her the story of the fire and how Bertha died. He also reveals that, although Rochester did not die, "many think he had better be dead". He lost a hand and is now blind. Jane immediately sets off for Ferndean where Rochester now lives.

- The journey to Thornfield Hall takes place over three pages, which allows the reader to experience Jane's thoughts about her return in detail. It also helps to build suspense.
- In addition, the account of the fire from Rochester's former butler draws out the tension.
- The fire is symbolic of the danger of passion, and his attempt to save Bertha shows that Rochester has changed for the better.

Volume 3, Chapter 11

Jane arrives late in the evening. She sees Rochester come out of the house and notes that 'in his countenance [she] saw a change'. Eventually, she approaches the house and takes Rochester's candle in to him.

To begin with, he does not believe that she is really there: "It is a dream". She reveals that she is now a woman of independent means and that she can "build a house of my own close up to your door".

They talk and she teases him as she used to do, even allowing him to feel jealous of her relationship with St. John. She tells him that "if you wish me to love you, could you but see how much I *do* love you, you would be proud and content. All my heart is yours, sir: it belongs to you".

He asks her to marry him and she agrees. He tells her of a night when he "asked of God, at once in anguish and humility, if I had not been long enough desolate, afflicted, tormented; and might not soon taste bliss and peace once more". Jane realizes that it was this same night when she heard 'the mysterious summons' which called her to his side.

- It is Jane who is now in control. She has been freed by her financial independence.

> **Key quotations**
>
> "Great God!—what delusion has come over me? What sweet madness has seized me?"
>
> [...] in his presence I thoroughly lived; and he lived in mine.
>
> His countenance reminded one of a lamp quenched, waiting to be relit [...]
>
> "You are no ruin, sir—no lightning-struck tree [...]"

Volume 3, Chapter 12: Conclusion

This chapter picks up the story ten years later. Jane and Rochester are now married. She tells the reader that Adèle felt 'frantic joy' at seeing Jane again.

Jane talks of the pleasure that she has found in marriage to Rochester: 'All my confidence is bestowed on him; all his confidence is devoted to me: we are precisely suited in character; perfect concord is the result.' She also reveals

Activity 9

1. Copy the extract below and add annotations to the **highlighted** words to show what Brontë's language reveals about the relationship between Jane and Rochester at this point in the novel.

Jane is the active subject in this sentence, suggesting her dominance.

I **took** that **dear** hand, held it a moment to my lips, then **let it pass** round my shoulder: being so much lower of stature than he, **I served** both for his **prop** and **guide**. **We entered the wood, and wended homeward**.

Suggests that she is beneath him in the hierarchy.

2. Now think back to Jane and Rochester's relationship earlier in the novel. How does this differ? Find quotations from earlier in the novel to support your answer.

3. What has been the catalyst for this change in their relationship?

that, within two years of their marriage, Rochester's sight began to return and they felt that **'God had tempered judgment with mercy'** when he is able to see their son.

* All of the major characters' stories are concluded satisfactorily.

* Jane's intention to become a governess again is not met as her **'time and cares were now required by another'**. Although it is clear that she is very happy in her relationship, it could be said that her independence has once again been taken from her.

* It is revealed that St. John is dying but that **'No fear of death will darken St. John's last hour: his mind will be unclouded; his heart will be undaunted; his hope will be sure; his faith steadfast'**.

Activity 10

1. **'Reader, I married him.'** Is this a satisfactory conclusion to Jane and Rochester's relationship? Is it believable? Explain your views with evidence from the text.

2. In Volume 1, Chapter 11, Jane describes her life as having **'its flowers and pleasures, as well as its thorns and toils'**.

   * Thinking about the novel as a whole, make a list of the 'flowers and pleasures' and another of the 'thorns and toils' in Jane's life.

   * Overall, do you think Jane's life experiences have been mainly positive or negative? Explain why, giving evidence from the text to support your answer.

Structure

As well as being divided into chapters, the novel falls into three parts, each of which deals with a different phase of Jane's life. Some sections of the novel follow on chronologically, while in other places there are significant gaps in the timeline.

At the start of the novel, Jane is just ten years old. By the end of the novel, she is a grown woman, married with a child of her own.

Activity 11

1. As you read the novel, copy and complete the first three columns of the table below to show the main events in each part of the narrative. Make sure that you cover the key events, but don't try to cover everything!

Section	Chapter	Key events	Time
Volume 1	1	• Jane is introduced • She argues with John and is sent to the red room	
	2	• She thinks she sees the ghost of her dead uncle • Mrs Reed insists on punishing her further • She faints	Later that day

2. Next, complete the 'Time' column, looking for clues in the text about when each event took place.

3. In some parts of the novel, there are large gaps in the narrative. Why do you think Brontë left these gaps? Does this add to or detract from the story as a whole?

Dramatic structure

The novel is divided into three volumes of unequal length, but it can also be divided into five parts, each of which is based in a different setting: Gateshead, Lowood, Thornfield Hall, Moor House and Ferndean.

Jane Eyre also follows a traditional structure for dramatic works, which looks like this:

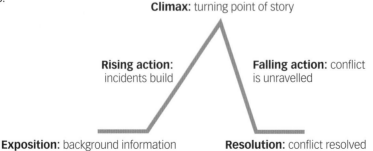

Climax: turning point of story

Rising action: incidents build

Falling action: conflict is unravelled

Exposition: background information

Resolution: conflict resolved

Activity 12

1. Copy the diagram and mark on it where each of the five settings appear in the story. This will help you to understand the structure of the novel.

2. Why do you think Brontë decided to structure the novel in this way? What do you think this structure adds to our understanding of the narrative?

Foreshadowing

Foreshadowing is a literary device used to hint at events to come later in the narrative, which can help to create suspense. One key example of foreshadowing in *Jane Eyre* is when Jane reveals that she thinks she has "some poor, low relations called Eyre" in Volume 1, Chapter 3, which eventually leads to her **inheritance** later in the story:

Activity 13

1. With a partner, think about what other events are foreshadowed within the novel. Create a chain of events for each of them.

2. How does Brontë's use of foreshadowing help structure her narrative?

> **inheritance** the property, money and title of a person who dies, which can be given to someone else

Writing about plot and structure

Upgrade

In an assessment, you will need to show an appreciation of how the writer develops ideas and characters throughout the novel. You will also need to show that you understand the key events and why they happen.

Make sure that you understand:

- how the plot develops, including how Brontë has chosen to structure the novel

- how Brontë has used techniques such as foreshadowing to introduce ideas and create suspense.

Biography of Charlotte Brontë

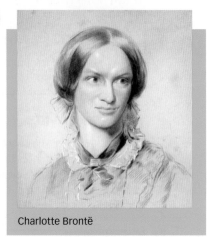

- Charlotte Brontë, born in 1816, was one of six children. She had four sisters (Maria, Elizabeth, Emily and Anne) and one brother (Branwell).

- Later in life, Charlotte, Emily and Anne became successful writers. Branwell wrote and painted but was not particularly successful. He eventually became an alcoholic and opium addict, and died at the age of 31.

- Charlotte's father, Patrick Brontë, was a clergyman in the village of Haworth in Yorkshire.

- In 1821, her mother died of cancer and left the children in the care of their aunt and father.

Charlotte Brontë

They were sent to the Clergy Daughters' School at Cowan Bridge, a strict Christian school. There the two older sisters, Maria and Elizabeth, caught the **tuberculosis** that killed them.

- After that the other children were kept at home for a time. During this period, Charlotte helped to teach her younger siblings.

- After several jobs as a governess, Charlotte returned home. She and her sisters decided to set up their own school. She went to study in Brussels, Belgium, in 1842 with her sister Emily and remained there until 1844.

- Their plans to set up a school failed, but in 1846 the sisters published their first collection of poems under the **pseudonyms** of Ellis, Currer and Acton Bell. Charlotte later stated that this was because:

> Averse to personal publicity, we veiled our own names under those of Currer, Ellis and Acton Bell; the ambiguous choice being dictated by a sort of conscientious scruple at assuming Christian names positively masculine, while we did not like to declare ourselves women, because — without at that time suspecting that our mode of writing and thinking was not what is called 'feminine' — we had a vague impression that authoresses are liable to be looked on with prejudice […]

- In 1848, the sisters revealed their identities to their publisher. In the same year, Branwell and Emily died.

pseudonym a 'pen name'; the name a writer uses so they don't have to use their real name

tuberculosis a highly infectious disease characterized by excessive and persistent coughing

- Charlotte became a part of literary society in the late 1840s and early 1850s.

- In 1852, Charlotte received a proposal of marriage from the curate of her father's church, which she and her father turned down. Two years later, he proposed again and they were married in 1854.

- In 1855, while pregnant, Charlotte caught pneumonia and died.

As a child, Brontë understood the need for an education for herself and worked hard to make good progress at school. She worked as a teacher for a short time, but did not enjoy it. So she attempted to make a success of her writing. When that did not receive the response she desired, she went back to teaching. Brontë continued to write while she worked as a governess. Despite not feeling fulfilled in her work as an educator, she continued to take it seriously, feeling a sense of responsibility to her family.

Tips for assessment

You should only mention the author's background in relation to how it may affect what Brontë wrote in the text.

Activity 1

Look at the information about Charlotte Brontë and her family. How has Brontë used events from her own life experiences in her novel? Why do you think that she chose to do this?

Historical and social context

Social class

Poverty in Victorian England meant a hard, and often shortened, life

Victorian England followed a rigid class system and many people made judgements about others based on their class. As a clergyman, Brontë's father was a member of the upper middle class. However, his work would also have brought him into contact with the working class and the underclass.

Jane Eyre focuses on the lives of the middle classes, but references are also made to the working-class poor. Even though Jane is very unhappy with the Reed family, she does not want to live with what Mrs Reed calls her **"poor, low relations"** because 'poverty for me was synonymous with degradation' (*Volume 1, Chapter 3*).

Activity 2

Jane's attitude to the poor alters over the course of the novel. How does it change and what causes her attitude to change?

Although Jane is from a middle-class family, she is considered by the Reeds to be of lower status because she has no money of her own. As an orphan, she is dependent on the kindness of others. As Bessie reminds her, **"you are under obligations to Mrs. Reed: she keeps you; if she were to turn you off, you would have to go to the poor-house"** *(Volume 1, Chapter 2)*.

Inheritance and wealth

Victorian rules of inheritance also play a part in Jane's status. The eldest son of a family would usually inherit the bulk of the family estate. Other children would have to either marry someone wealthy or become financially independent through a career. Employment opportunities were extremely limited for Victorian women, so not many were able to work to become financially independent.

Since women did not have the same access to education as their male peers, they were reliant on men for support. A husband was therefore required. Marriage also meant that women could become mothers and focus on the running of a household, which was considered the natural 'sphere' for a woman. The woman had to take a **dowry** from her father into the marriage. The amount of money depended on the wealth of her **fiancé's** family, not the wealth of her own family. This stopped most women from marrying above their class.

During the 18th and early 19th centuries, a woman had to give up her financial independence upon her marriage. Once married, all her wealth and possessions became her husband's property. She had to get her husband's permission to give money or valuable possessions away, even in her own will. Even during the engagement, her finances were linked to her fiancé's, who had the final say about what she could spend her money on. In 1882, the Married Women's Property Act gave married women much more financial freedom.

Unmarried women were able to keep control of their own finances, including leaving their wealth or possessions to anyone they chose – often other single women in their family. In this way unmarried women, such as Charlotte Brontë and her sisters, were able to achieve some financial independence. Jane benefits from her uncle's will in such a way.

Activity 3

Think about the timeline for Jane's inheritance from John Eyre and the information above about money and inheritance. Why does Brontë have Jane come into money when she does in the novel? What does it mean about her ability to keep control of the money?

The position of women

The **Industrial Revolution** meant that working-class women could become more independent through employment in the factories. However, single middle-class women still lacked that freedom. The only occupation open to them was that of governess. The role of a governess, while respectable, was insecure. A governess was not treated as one of the family that employed her, but neither was she one of the servants. This meant that governesses were often treated badly but were powerless to do anything about it.

Anne Brontë wrote a novel that focused on the treatment of governesses – *Agnes Grey* (1847) – and many people believe that she based it on her own experiences.

Victorian women had few civil or political rights and were unable to vote. Charlotte Brontë believed that women should not be given the right to vote, but she did think that they should be able to use their talents rather than simply staying at home and 'making puddings and knitting stockings' *(Volume 1, Chapter 12).*

Activity 4

Look at the extract below. What does it tell us about Brontë's view of the position of women in society? There are some notes to help you.

Although she says 'human beings', the context suggests women. They are not content to sit around as expected to.

She suggests some women are in a worse position because they are able to do less than her.

Women need to use their brains.

It is in vain to say human beings ought to be satisfied with tranquillity: they must have action; and they will make it if they cannot find it. Millions are condemned to a stiller doom than mine, and millions are in silent revolt against their lot. Nobody knows how many rebellions besides political rebellions ferment in the masses of life which people earth. Women are supposed to be very calm generally: but women feel just as men feel; they need exercise for their faculties, and a field for their efforts as much as their brothers do; they suffer from too rigid a restraint, too absolute a stagnation, precisely as men would suffer; and it is narrow-minded in their more privileged fellow-creatures to say that they ought to confine themselves to making puddings and knitting stockings, to playing on the piano and embroidering bags. It is thoughtless to condemn them, or laugh at them, if they seek to do more or learn more than custom has pronounced necessary for their sex. *(Volume 1, Chapter 12)*

---

dowry money paid by the father of the bride to the groom when a couple marry

fiancé the man a woman is engaged to marry

Industrial Revolution the period from about 1760 when goods began to be made in factories, giving many more people the opportunity for employment

Madness

The Victorian era marked a change in attitude towards mental illness. Previously, people who suffered from mental illness were kept in large 'lunatic asylums'. These were much like prisons, designed to ensure that patients could not escape. By 1842, following a new law which required all asylums to be inspected, institutions which kept patients locked away and did not attempt to treat them were considered inhumane and widely criticized. Although there was little understanding of the causes of madness, there was a move towards trying to find cures. In 1848, a doctor from an asylum in Middlesex wrote that:

> The whole of the **barbarous** system of **coercion** and restraint [...] was founded on a **fallacy**, and that insanity [...] is simply a state of unsound, physical health – a state of functional disease – in the great majority of cases capable of a cure, under appropriate treatment; capable also, under **injudicious** treatment, of being **rendered** permanent and incurable.

While many people were forcibly admitted to mental institutions, wealthy families were able to choose to have their mentally ill relatives admitted in order to receive treatment.

It was generally believed that women were more prone to madness than men: the word 'hysteria' is linked to the Latin word for womb.

Activity 5

Look again at the description of Bertha's room in Volume 2, Chapter 11. What does Brontë's description suggest about Mr Rochester's attitude to mental illness?

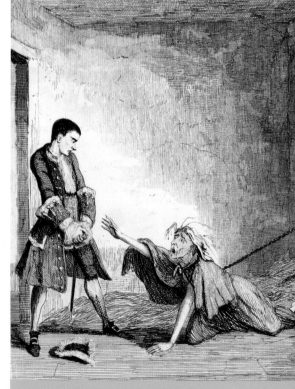

Those suspected of having a mental illness were treated in hospital

barbarous cruel

coercion pressure

fallacy false or mistaken belief

injudicious careless and badly informed

rendered made

Religion

Religion was of enormous significance in the Victorian period. Many people thought that religious belief and living a Christian life would bring an end to poverty and **immorality**, which were thought to be linked. People went to church regularly and, in villages and small towns, the church was central to the community.

The Church of England was the state church, but other **denominations** were increasing in number at this time. The **Evangelical movement**, in particular, was growing: its focus on charity and missionary work was central to its ideals.

> ## Activity 6
>
> 1. Study the following characters in the novel. What attitudes to religion do each of them reflect?
>
>   - Mr Brocklehurst
>   - St. John Rivers
>   - Helen Burns
>   - Eliza Reed
>
> 2. What do these differing attitudes, and Brontë's own experiences, suggest to us about her views on religion?

Education

The novel contains two distinct types of education: taught by governess within the home and taught in school. Each is presented quite differently.

Lowood is thought to be based on Brontë's own experiences at Cowan Bridge School. Below is an extract from a report of her time at the school:

> Charlotte Brontë. Entered August 10, 1824. Writes indifferently. **Ciphers** a little, and works neatly. Knows nothing of grammar, geography, history, or **accomplishments**. Altogether clever of her age, but knows nothing systematically (at eight years old!). Left school June 1, 1825 – Governess.

accomplishments pastimes, such as painting, singing, dancing, playing the piano and speaking a foreign language, considered desirable for a young lady

cipher *(or cypher)* to solve basic maths problems

denomination a religious group with a recognized name

Evangelical movement a religious movement that tries to convert others to its faith

immorality wicked behaviour

As **boarders**, the Brontës had to wear the 'charity children' uniform and were often humiliated by their treatment. Punishments at school included having to wear a dunce's cap or sit in isolation, being refused food and playtime, and **corporal punishment**. Charlotte's sisters Elizabeth and Maria died of tuberculosis contracted while at school.

Children wearing 'charity children' uniforms

Activity 7

Look again at the Lowood section of the novel (Chapters 5–10).

1. What evidence can you find that Brontë was influenced by her experiences at Cowan Bridge?

2. Expand on your answer.

- Make a list of all of the things that Jane learns in that part of the novel.

- Now divide them into two groups: personal lessons and social lessons.

- What does this suggest to you about the purpose of school at this time?

For women, education was seen as a means of escape from the limitations of their gender. By becoming educated, they could improve their marriage prospects, even if they could not become independent. Writing in 1839, Sarah Stickney Ellis noted that 'any woman of respectable education […], possessing a well-regulated mind, might move with ease and dignity into a higher sphere than that to which she has become accustomed'.

Of course, moving into a higher social class would rely on her also being able to find the dowry required by her fiancé's family.

Activity 8

What does the education of other female characters in the novel consist of? What does this suggest about the qualities that were considered valuable in women at the time? Write a paragraph explaining your ideas, with close reference to the text.

As well as formal education, the novel includes many examples of education through experience. For example, Jane's religious and moral education is influenced by her friend Helen Burns.

Activity 9

What do you think is the most important type of education presented in the novel – moral, religious or formal (school) education? Explain your answer with evidence from the text.

Literary context

Fictional autobiography

Jane Eyre is presented to the reader as an **autobiography**. Although it is clear that Brontë was influenced in her writing by things that had happened in her own life, the novel is actually a work of fiction. A review at the time stated that 'taken as a novel or history of events, the book is obviously defective; but as an analysis of a single mind [...] it may claim comparison with any work of the same species'.

Activity 10

Do you agree that *Jane Eyre* is a good 'analysis of a single mind'? Do you think that Brontë's portrayal of Jane over the course of the novel is an effective 'autobiography'? Explain why.

Bildungsroman and the sentimental

A **Bildungsroman** is a 'coming-of-age' novel, in which the main character undergoes moral development throughout the narrative. A Bildungsroman generally follows a specific structure:

- At the beginning of the novel, the main character is inexperienced. The novel focuses on their moral development.
- There is an incident that sets the **protagonist** on their journey of discovery.

autobiography literally means 'writing the self'; a true account of someone's life from their own point of view

Bildungsroman a coming-of-age novel in which the main character grows up and develops moral judgement

boarders students who stayed overnight at the school, as well as going for lessons

corporal punishment being caned or smacked

protagonist main character

- During the journey, the protagonist undergoes many trials and problems, and will fail several times. They have to fight against the boundaries placed upon them by society.
- There will be a moment of clarity when they realize what they need to do in order to be satisfied.
- In the end they accept the rules of society.
- At the end of the novel, there may not be a clear sense of what will happen next.

Activity 11

Using the structure of a Bildungsroman novel above, identify each of the six structural elements in *Jane Eyre*. Include quotations to support your ideas.

Sentimental novels were written to evoke an emotional response from readers and focused on feelings rather than action. People believed that an ability to show their feelings showed strength of character.

Activity 12

Do you think that *Jane Eyre* can be characterized as a sentimental novel? Give examples from the text to support your answer.

The gothic

The **gothic genre** has its origins in the 1700s and has continued to be a very popular form of writing until the present day. Traditionally, gothic texts have certain features in common, including:

- isolated buildings
- mysterious happenings
- helpless women
- strong and powerful men
- elements of the **supernatural**
- secrets
- frightening weather.

> **genre** a literary category such as comedy, tragedy, romance
>
> **gothic** a type of fiction that includes references to death and fear, but also to nature and emotion
>
> **sentimental novel** a type of fiction written to evoke an emotional response
>
> **supernatural** ghosts and other creatures that do not belong to the natural world

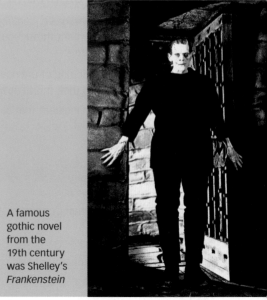

A famous gothic novel from the 19th century was Shelley's *Frankenstein*

Activity 13

1. Which of the gothic features listed above can be found in *Jane Eyre*?

2. Why do you think Brontë chose to include gothic features in her novel? What do they add to the narrative? Discuss your ideas with a partner.

Many gothic novels were written by women and some people think that this style of writing allowed them to express their fears about marriage in an acceptable way. Often, gothic novels included male characters who could be described as 'mad, bad and dangerous to know' – a reference to Lord Byron, who was well known for his scandalous behaviour.

Activity 14

Matthew Arnold, a Victorian author and critic, wrote: 'Miss Brontë has written a hideous, undelightful, convulsed, constricted novel […] one of the most utterly disagreeable books I've ever read […] [because] the writer's mind contains nothing but hunger, rebellion and rage and therefore that is all she can, in fact, put in her book'.

- Find as many examples as you can of 'hunger' (not just relating to food), 'rebellion' and 'rage' in the novel.

- Now think about why Matthew Arnold might have thought that these examples made *Jane Eyre* a 'hideous' book. Why might his attitude to life have been different from Brontë's?

Writing about context

Upgrade

Although your question might not directly mention the word 'context', remember to show that you understand the context and can relate it to the question. You must ensure that you don't just write down facts about the writer or about the position of women in society, but instead clearly relate them to the text. For example, if you were asked about Brontë's presentation of Jane in the novel, you might want to write about the fact that she is a governess. You might write:

Jane is a governess and is therefore on the boundaries of two social groups. She is neither a servant, who Mrs Fairfax reminds Jane "are only servants, and one can't

Shows understanding of the context.

converse with them on terms of equality: one must keep them at due distance, for fear of losing one's authority" *(Volume 1, Chapter 11)*, nor a member of the family. As a middle-class woman, she is on the same social level as the family, but the fact that she needs to work for a living puts her on the same level as the servants. This causes her both practical and emotional difficulties...

Giving an example from the novel here would help to link the text to the context.

Main characters

There are a number of characters in *Jane Eyre* but only three are developed to emerge as 'main' characters. The remainder all play important parts in the story, but they act to help the reader discover more about the nature of the main characters and to develop the story.

Jane Eyre

Jane Eyre, our eponymous heroine, is the first character that we meet in the novel. She immediately

Jane is the heroine in the novel

presents herself as an outsider in the Reed family, **'humbled by the consciousness of my physical inferiority to Eliza, John, and Georgiana Reed'** *(Volume 1, Chapter 1)*. As an orphan, she is of lowly status and is treated poorly by her aunt both at the start of the novel and later, when Jane returns to visit her on her deathbed. Described as a **"queer, frightened, shy little thing"** *(Volume 1, Chapter 4)* by the nursemaid Bessie, Jane is tyrannized by her elder cousin John. When she loses her temper and fights him she is locked in the room where her uncle died and suffers a fit. This is the first point of development for Jane's character. Her loss of control and passionate response to the events is the catalyst for change in her life.

Sent away to school, a place which she hopes will be **'a complete change: [...] an entrance into a new life'** *(Volume 1, Chapter 3)*, she is able for the first time to make a friend. However, life at Lowood is often unpleasant, and there are times when she suffers greatly – physically and mentally. This is one of the most important parts of her life in terms of the lessons that she learns. The characters of Helen Burns and Miss Temple exert an important, positive influence on her personal and religious development. Mr Brocklehurst provides Jane with an interesting contrast to these truly **pious** teachings. His hypocritical and hard-hearted behaviour ensures Jane retains some scepticism about the world around her. Jane begins to develop reason to moderate her childish passion.

Later, she goes to Thornfield Hall where she finds fulfilment in her work as a governess for Adèle and encounters Mr Rochester. She continues to develop as a character, and grow in depth, showing more restraint in her behaviour as she grows older and becomes less impulsive. During this time Jane demonstrates a complex

pious religious

combination of deference, submission and confidence as a character. She grows in boldness during her interactions with Rochester, yet maintains a deferential demeanour with other characters as befitting a governess. She also recognizes her position in the family as a somewhat isolated and dependent one: "a solitary dependent in a great house" *(Volume 2, Chapter 4)*, and determines to ensure that she has a measure of independence to prevent her being treated like the property of Rochester once they are engaged: "I never can bear being dressed like a doll by Mr. Rochester" *(Volume 2, Chapter 9)*.

Activity 1

1. In order for characters to have depth and seem realistic, there are certain elements a writer needs to consider when creating characters:
   - **Background:** Where do they come from?
   - **Appearance:** What do they look like?
   - **Relationships:** Who are their friends/ family? How do they interact with others?
   - **Speech:** What do they sound like when they speak to others? What do they sound like when they speak directly to the reader?
   - **Ambition:** What do they want from life?
   - **Flaws:** What faults do they have?
   - **Difficulties:** What do they have to overcome to achieve their ambitions?

2. Looking at the elements above, write notes on how Brontë has developed Jane's character over the course of the novel. Use short quotations to help you.

3. Using ideas from your notes to help you, do you think that Jane is a well-developed character? Explain why.

Tips for assessment

When you are writing about characters, it will help you to improve your answers if you understand the role the minor characters play in the development of the main characters. Some of the minor characters are less well developed, for example you know very little of Miss Temple's life before Lowood, but this does not affect her pivotal role in Jane's life as her mentor and confidante. You must ensure you analyse the purpose of a character when you include them in your answer and draw out how they act as a device to the plot.

Leaving Thornfield Hall is a physical step towards independence, although Jane's motives are initially just to escape her relationship with Rochester after the revelations about Bertha. She acknowledges "All is changed about me, sir; I must change too". Up to this point, she has obeyed Rochester's wishes; leaving Thornfield marks an important development in their relationship, in that she directly asserts her independence. She finds sanctuary in the household of the Rivers family where she begins this final change in her character. She develops independence as she runs a schoolroom and continues a life away from Thornfield; however, her love for Rochester continues to influence her decisions and outlook on life. The proposal of marriage from St. John Rivers has nothing to do with love; it is formed as a Christian duty, and during her deliberations of whether to accept him Jane realizes that while she wants to be independent, she also wants to be loved and to express her love.

> **Key quotations**
>
> [...] forced to keep the fire of my nature continually low, to compel it to burn inwardly and never utter a cry, though the imprisoned flame consumed vital after vital—*this* would be unendurable.
> *(Volume 3, Chapter 8)*

The conclusion of Jane's character development is to trust her heart, and to pursue Rochester. Now also financially independent with an inheritance, Jane is finally in control of herself, her emotions and her destiny. She is able to marry Rochester for love rather than for position, and to have achieved her highest ambition while staying true to her character's values.

Activity 2

Within *Jane Eyre*, Brontë uses the **binary opposites** of passion and reason to develop many of her characters, including Jane herself.

1. For each of the quotations below, decide which show passion and which show reason.

   - '[...] my soul began to expand, to exult, with the strangest sense of freedom, of triumph, I ever felt.' *(Volume 1, Chapter 4)*
   - 'I resolved in the depth of my heart that I would be most moderate [...]' *(Volume 1, Chapter 8)*
   - "while I breathe and think, I must love him." *(Volume 2, Chapter 2)*
   - 'I could not, in those days, see God for his creature: of whom I had made an idol.' *(Volume 2, Chapter 9)*
   - "I am ready to go to India, if I may go free." *(Volume 3, Chapter 8)*
   - "I will be your neighbour, your nurse, your housekeeper. I find you lonely: I will be your companion [...]" *(Volume 3, Chapter 11)*

2. With a partner, find as many other examples of passion and reason as you can in relation to Jane and her thoughts and actions. In the end, do you think Jane is more driven by passion or reason? Explain why, with close reference to the text.

3. Now think about the other major characters in the novel. Which are driven by passion and which by reason? What do you think that Brontë's message to her reader about passion and reason is? Explain why.

I know what it is to live entirely for and with what I love best on earth. *(Volume 3, Conclusion)*

My Edward and I, then, are happy: and the more so, because those we most love are happy likewise. *(Volume 3, Conclusion)*

As a narrator, Jane is looking back on her own childhood and the focus of the novel is always on her thoughts and feelings. This means that anything she tells the reader is coloured by her particular view of the world, and is not necessarily **unbiased**.

Activity 3

Look closely at the extract below:

Her childish view.

Judges them and sees them as inferior.

> Poverty looks grim to grown people; still more so to children: they have not much idea of industrious, working, respectable poverty; they think of the word only as connected with ragged clothes, scanty food, fireless grates, rude manners and debasing vices: poverty for me was synonymous with degradation. [...] I could not see how poor people had the means of being kind; and then to learn to speak like them, to adopt their manners, to be uneducated, to grow up like one of the poor women I saw sometimes nursing their children or washing their clothes at the cottage doors of the village of Gateshead [...].
> *(Volume 1, Chapter 3)*

As a child, she sees "poor people" as being different from her.

1. On your own copy of the extract, add your own notes to show Jane's attitudes to poverty. Use one colour to continue to identify her attitudes as a child and a different colour to identify her attitudes as an adult.

2. Think about why Charlotte Brontë presented Jane as having these views. What did she intend the reader to understand about poverty?

binary opposites things which are totally opposite, for example, hot and cold

unbiased balanced viewpoint, fair and accurate

I had meant to be so good, and to do so much at Lowood; to make so many friends, to earn respect, and win affection. *(Volume 1, Chapter 8)*

"I will not be your English Céline Varens." *(Volume 2, Chapter 9)*

To have yielded then would have been an error of principle; to have yielded now would have been an error of judgment. *(Volume 3, Chapter 9)*

Activity 4

Think about the other female characters in the novel. Some of them have a great deal of influence over Jane, while others share similarities in their nature.

1. Copy and complete the table below to show these connections. Add quotations to support your ideas.

Character	Relationship with Jane	Quotation
Miss Temple	Teaches Jane the importance of role, function and conforming to society's expectations – she does not argue with Mr Brocklehurst over the extra breakfast and hair cutting. She clearly does not agree with him, but acts upon his wishes when he is present.	
Helen Burns		
Mrs Reed		
Georgiana and Eliza Reed		
Bessie		
Mrs Fairfax		
Blanche Ingram		
Diana and Mary Rivers		
Bertha Mason	Both have passionate natures – she reflects Jane's passionate side and the danger that is to be found in acting upon emotion alone.	

2. By the end of the novel it could be argued Jane has become a fully developed character. How have these relationships influenced her development? Would the absence of one have made her character more or less believable? Explain why with evidence from the text.

Tips for assessment

It is important to remember that when you are asked about the characters in the novel, you must write about them as characters, not as real people. You need to think about why Charlotte Brontë presented each of them in the way that she did, and what methods she uses to guide our responses.

Activity 5

Exam questions will often ask you to write about how characters change over the course of the novel. To do this effectively, you will need to be able to write about what changes and why.

Copy the table below and complete it in as much detail as you can. It will help you when you come to revise. You could also do it for other characters.

Volume/ Chapter	What Jane is like	Why she is like that	Key quotation
Volume 1, Chapter 1	frightened and lonely	She is bullied by John and no-one ever seems to see what he does to her.	
Volume 1, Chapter 2			I dared commit no fault: I strove to fulfil every duty; and I was termed naughty and tiresome, sullen and sneaking, from morning to noon, and from noon to night.

Tips for assessment

It is vital to be able to write about how the characters in *Jane Eyre* change and develop over the course of the novel. Creating a timeline for each character will help with this.

Edward Rochester

Most of the reader's views of Rochester are presented in the light of Jane's feelings for him. A man of means who offers Jane employment when she leaves Lowood, ultimately he offers her his heart and a home.

The reader's first introduction to Rochester is presented as a direct contrast to that of Jane. Unlike Jane's timid, physical inferiority, Rochester rides into view and creates a strong and dominant impression 'of middle height and considerable breadth of chest' *(Volume 1, Chapter 12)*. Brontë does not portray him as a typical tall, dark and handsome hero, yet he is darkly striking and Jane reacts more favourably towards him because of this than had he been 'handsome, heroic-looking [...] smiled and been good-humoured' *(Volume 1, Chapter 12)*.

Mr Rochester (*Jane Eyre*, 2011)

> **Key quotations**
>
> He had a dark face, with stern features and a heavy brow; his eyes and gathered eyebrows looked ireful and thwarted just now; he was past youth, but had not reached middle age: perhaps he might be thirty-five. *(Volume 1, Chapter 12)*

From his first appearance in Volume 1, Chapter 12, Rochester is consistent in his character: 'the frown, the roughness' Jane observes is his usual manner towards everyone. However, this disguises a layer of gentleness which is revealed only in his relationship with Jane, and makes him more appealing to the reader. Indeed, their first meeting begins with an instance of physical weakness when he falls from his horse beside her, which could be regarded as a **metaphor** for their future relationship – Jane makes him confront his weaknesses.

His relationship with Jane is unconventional: as a governess she is only just above a servant in his home and yet he treats her very much as an equal. In their conversations, she holds her own in their verbal sparring matches, and he has to learn to treat her with respect: 'when summoned by formal invitation to his presence, I was honoured by a cordiality of reception that made me feel I really possessed the power to amuse him' *(Volume 1, Chapter 15)*. Rochester observes that "I wish to be a better man than I have been; than I am" *(Volume 1, Chapter 15)*. Although he does not direct this towards Jane, it is clear that his character begins to change once he has met her – and that she (albeit unknowingly) provides the impetus for his change. However, his treatment of women leaves something to be desired: he uses Blanche to test Jane's feelings for him; marries Bertha for her money and then confines her to the attic; takes mistresses in Europe and then suggests that, since he cannot marry her, Jane should also become a mistress. It is through his direct speech that we learn most about his attitudes to women.

> **metaphor** a comparison of one thing to another to make a description more vivid; unlike a simile, it does not use the words 'like' or 'as'

Activity 6

Look closely at the extracts below:

He clearly assumes that she will. →

Why would this give him the right to be "masterful"? →

"do you agree with me that I have a right to be a little masterful, abrupt; perhaps exacting, sometimes, on the grounds I stated: namely, that I am old enough to be your father, and that I have battled through a varied experience with many men of many nations, and roamed over half the globe, while you have lived quietly with one set of people in one house?" *(Volume 1, Chapter 14)* ←

The juxtaposition of the three verbs suggests that his activities have been more dynamic than hers, and that this gives him the right to tell her what to do.

What does the fact that he doesn't tell her himself suggest about him? →

"I caused a rumour to reach [Blanche Ingram] that my fortune was not a third of what was supposed, and after that I presented myself to see the result: it was coldness both from her and her mother. I would not—I could not—marry Miss Ingram. You—you strange—you almost unearthly thing!—I love as my own flesh. You—poor and obscure, and small and plain as you are—I entreat to accept me as a husband." *(Volume 2, Chapter 8)*

For whom? →

"It was a grovelling fashion of existence: I should never like to return to it. Hiring a mistress is the next worse thing to buying a slave: both are often by nature, and always by position, inferior; and to live familiarly with inferiors is degrading. I now hate the recollection of the time I passed with Céline, Giacinta, and Clara." *(Volume 3, Chapter 1)*

1. On your own copy of each extract, annotate it to show what each of these examples reveals about Rochester and his attitudes. Try to think beyond that which is most obvious, using the questions beside the extracts to help you.

2. Why do you think that Brontë chose to present Rochester in this way? Think about your work on character analysis so far, and consider how the main character Jane has reacted to him as he is.

Although Rochester is not often charming, he is something of a **sympathetic character**. He was tricked into marrying Bertha and lost his share of his fortune due to his brother's scheming: "his spirit could not brook what he had to suffer" *(Volume 1, Chapter 14)*. Brontë suggests he fell into a life of debauchery after he was betrayed and this is given as justification for some of his behaviour, and explanation for why he developed into such a self-motivated character.

This character undergoes a significant development because of his association with Jane, yet he does not initially change his way of thinking or belief in his own superiority. In one conversation with Jane he observes "you, with your gravity, considerateness, and caution were made to be the recipient of secrets" *(Volume 1, Chapter 15)*. However, although he relates in detail his past sexual liaisons, he does not entrust Jane with the details of his marriage to Bertha until he is forced to by circumstance. His attempt to marry Jane bigamously demonstrates he was still acting selfishly, as he had in all his relationships with women.

It is certain Rochester does love Jane, but exactly how is open to interpretation. Rochester is passionate, and makes wild and varying declarations to describe Jane: "my second self, and best earthly companion", "you strange—you almost unearthly thing", "small and plain" *(Volume 2, Chapter 8)*, "radiant hazel eyes" *(Volume 2, Chapter 9)*. Brontë does not allow the reader to easily conclude Rochester is a selfish lover – he is clearly tormented by the wrong of his actions, even as he seeks to justify them in a delirious passage in Volume 2, Chapter 8: "I know my Maker sanctions what I do [...] For man's opinion—I defy it". However, it is with a certain coldness that, even as he proposes to Jane, he declares "that is the best of it" in response to her saying she has no relations to interfere.

Rochester is heartbroken by Jane's departure. After Thornfield is destroyed and he is injured he is physically broken too. By the end of the novel, Rochester has lost his sight and his independence: "He is now helpless, indeed—blind and a cripple" *(Volume 3, Chapter 11)* and is reliant on others. It is only by having his circumstances reduced and accepting responsibility for his actions that he is redeemed for his past behaviour: "I did wrong: I would have sullied my innocent flower [...] of late—I began to see and acknowledge the hand of God in my doom. I began to experience remorse, **repentance**; the wish for reconcilement to my Maker" *(Volume 3, Chapter 11)*. Brontë uses Rochester to make a powerful assertion about the truth of God and religious belief in the novel, and it is key to his final transformation into a man who is forgiven for his actions, and thus deserves Jane, a son and his sight.

infidelity unfaithfulness
repentance feeling of regret
sympathetic character someone the reader can feel sympathy for or care about

Activity 7

Consider the relationships that Rochester has or describes with the following characters over the course of the novel:

- Bertha Rochester
- Céline Varens
- Giacinta and Clara
- Blanche Ingram
- Adèle
- Mrs Fairfax
- Jane

1. Which relationships are strong, which are weak and which are broken at the end of the novel?

2. Add quotations to each of the relationships to support your ideas.

Although we tend to think of passion as a positive emotion, it can also be a negative one: the initial "grande passion" that Rochester feels for Céline is replaced by another form of passion – "the green snake of jealousy" (Volume 1, Chapter 15) when he discovers her **infidelity**. This strong and spontaneous emotion is replaced, eventually, by a more controlled approach when he agrees to give her daughter, Adèle, a home. This suggests that he begins to learn the danger of passion. However, this is tested in his relationship with Jane, and in giving in to passion again in trying to marry Jane bigamously, Brontë shows us its negativity because it results in Rochester's loss of Jane.

Activity 8

1. Now think about the other characters with whom Rochester has changing relationships. Track through each one to explain how their relationships change.

2. For each of them, talk to a partner about what the changing relationships reveal about Rochester as a character in the novel, as well as how they contribute to his development as a man. How do the quotations below show these changes?

Key quotations

"[...] he is very changeful and abrupt." (Volume 1, Chapter 13)

"When fate wronged me, I had not the wisdom to remain cool: I turned desperate; then I degenerated." (Volume 1, Chapter 14)

His idea was still with me; because it was not a vapour sunshine could disperse; nor a sand-traced effigy storms could wash away [...] (Volume 3, Chapter 8)

His countenance reminded one of a lamp quenched, waiting to be relit [...] (Volume 3, Chapter 11)

Violent as he had seemed in his despair, he, in truth, loved me far too well and too tenderly to constitute himself my tyrant [...] (Volume 3, Chapter 11)

Rochester is often considered to be an example of a Byronic hero: a character who is 'mad, bad, and dangerous to know', but who is all the more attractive for it. In literary terms, this means being:

> A man proud, moody, cynical, with defiance on his brow, and misery in his heart, a scorner of his kind, implacable in revenge, yet capable of deep and strong affection.   *Thomas Macanlay*

Activity 9

Thinking about the character of Rochester, do you agree that he is presented as a Byronic hero? Explain why with close reference to the text.

St. John Rivers

St. John (pronounced Sinjun) Rivers is devoted to his religion. He is absolutely motivated by genuine Christian **morality**, unlike Mr Brocklehurst, and puts his religion before himself, giving up on his love for Rosamond because she will not make a suitable wife for him. His proposal of marriage to Jane is a practical one rather than one based on romantic love: **"A missionary's wife you must— shall be. You shall be mine: I claim you—not for my pleasure, but for my Sovereign's service"** *(Volume 3, Chapter 8)*.

St. John is determined to have Jane as his wife

All of the decisions that he makes in life are based on his desire to serve his Master, and he often appears to be cold and unfeeling. His character flaw is that he is unable to see beyond his religious convictions, which leads him to see the world from a very restricted point of view. He tells Jane in Volume 3, Chapter 8 that she is **"formed for labour, not for love"** which suggests that he sees the world as involving a series of distinct choices rather than compromises: he **'lived only to aspire'** *(Volume 3, Chapter 8)* rather than wishing to be truly happy. For him, love is **'out of the question, [he] thought only of duty'** *(Volume 3, Chapter 9)*, which is what Jane intends to do when she leaves Rochester; however, through St. John, Brontë provides a very different interpretation of duty to consider.

Like Helen Burns, St. John believes that a better world awaits him after death: **'No fear of death will darken St. John's last hour: his mind will be unclouded; his heart will be undaunted; his hope will be sure; his faith steadfast'** *(Volume 3, Conclusion)*.

He is controlled and restrained in his behaviour, but **'not a man to be lightly refused'** *(Volume 3, Chapter 8)*. Despite being a man of religion, his behaviour is manipulative and self-righteous at times, and he looks down on those who do not share his high ideals.

> **Key quotations**
>
> "Refuse to be my wife, and you limit yourself for ever to a track of selfish ease and barren obscurity." *(Volume 3, Chapter 8)*

Activity 10

Look closely at the extract below in which Jane describes the first time that she heard St. John give a sermon:

The heart was thrilled, the mind astonished, by the power of the preacher: neither were softened. Throughout there was a strange bitterness; an absence of consolatory gentleness: stern allusions to Calvinistic doctrines—election, predestination, reprobation—were frequent; and each reference to these points sounded like a sentence pronounced for doom. *(Volume 3, Chapter 4)*

1. What does this description reveal about St. John Rivers's view of and attitude to religion?

2. In the preface to the novel, Brontë writes that **'Self-righteousness is not religion. […] narrow human doctrines […] should not be substituted for the world-redeeming creed of Christ.'** How does she show this attitude in her description of the sermon?

3. With a partner, find other examples of St. John's self-righteous attitude.

After Jane refuses his proposal, St. John refuses to even say goodnight to her, which upsets Jane: 'cordiality would not warm, nor tears move him' *(Volume 3, Chapter 8)*. When he attempts to persuade her again to marry him, Jane observes 'Oh, that gentleness! how far more potent is it than force! […] Yet I knew all the time, if I yielded now, I should not the less be made to repent, some day, of my former rebellion. His nature was not changed […] it was only elevated' *(Volume 3, Chapter 9)*. St. John is unrelenting in his pursuit of godliness, but unlike Mr Brocklehurst, he is as equally hard on himself as others.

> **Calvinist** a set of Christian beliefs based on the teachings of John Calvin. Calvinism stresses the moral weakness of humans
>
> **doctrines** rules
>
> **election** the idea that God chooses people to be saved based on whether He thinks they will have religious faith
>
> **morality** right and wrong, acting according to principle
>
> **predestination** the idea that God has already chosen some people to be saved, and that nothing can change that
>
> **reprobation** those who are not chosen will not be saved and will therefore be damned

Jane says that St. John 'had not yet found that peace of God which passeth all understanding' *(Volume 3, Chapter 4)* and he presents the idea of self-sacrifice as a step on his way to true religious service: he is prepared to give up on love with Rosamond in order to serve God.

His importance to Jane is reflected in the fact that Brontë gives him the last lines of the novel, devoted to his story, and revealing that he is expected to die soon. Although he readily accepts this fate, it is perhaps a reminder to the reader that this could also have been Jane's fate had she not rejected St. John's proposal in order to follow her heart and return to Rochester.

> **Key quotations**
>
> St. John was a good man; but I began to feel he had spoken truth of himself, when he said he was hard and cold. *(Volume 3, Chapter 8)*
>
> I found him a very patient, very forbearing, and yet an exacting master […] *(Volume 3, Chapter 8)*
>
> I am the servant of an infallible master. *(Volume 3, Chapter 8)*
>
> Firm, faithful, and devoted; full of energy, and zeal, and truth, he labours for his race […] *(Volume 3, Conclusion)*

Activity 11

In novels, different characters have different functions: they contribute different things to the telling of the story.

- **Protagonist:** The main character in the story. They have a problem of some kind to overcome, and the reader is expected to sympathize or empathize with them
- **Antagonist:** A major character who opposes the protagonist and puts obstacles in their way
- **Mentor:** A character who shows the lessons which the protagonist must learn in order to achieve their goal
- **Foil:** A character whose role is to highlight some aspect of another character's attitudes or beliefs
- **Dynamic:** A character who changes over time
- **Static:** A character who does not change over time
- **Minor characters:** Often included to help to move the plot forward

For each of the three characters discussed so far, talk to a partner about what their role is in the novel, and why they have been included. Think about:

- what they contribute to the action of the plot
- what they contribute to the presentation of Jane as a character
- whether they are well-developed characters.

Minor characters

Helen Burns

Helen appears in the novel for only a short time, but she has a lasting impact on Jane. She is her friend at Lowood and teaches her how to behave in a Christian way. Although her untidy drawers and dirty fingernails suggest that she is, at heart, as rebellious as Jane, she accepts her punishments without complaint. She believes in the Christian doctrine of 'turning the other cheek' (not retaliating when someone treats you badly) and encourages Jane to behave in the same way.

Her death from tuberculosis is inevitable, but she approaches it without fear. In fact, she accepts death as a part of life and believes that she will go to God: **"I can resign my immortal part to him without any misgiving. God is my father; God is my friend: I love him; I believe he loves me"** *(Volume 1, Chapter 9)*. Her religious belief is in strong contrast with that of Mr Brocklehurst.

> **Key quotations**
>
> She looks as if she were thinking of something beyond her punishment—beyond her situation: of something not round her nor before her. *(Volume 1, Chapter 6)*
>
> "Love your enemies; bless them that curse you; do good to them that hate you and despitefully use you." *(Volume 1, Chapter 6)*

Mr Brocklehurst

Mr Brocklehurst owns Lowood, the school to which the young Jane is sent. He claims to be a religious man, but he has a view of Christianity which is based on punishment and **oppression** and the pupils at Lowood endure much hardship: **"when you put bread and cheese, instead of burnt porridge into these children's mouths, you may indeed feed their vile bodies, but you little think how you starve their immortal souls!"** *(Volume 1, Chapter 7)*. He is a hypocrite, demanding that the girls in the school should **"clothe themselves with shame-facedness and sobriety, not with braided hair and costly apparel"** *(Volume 1, Chapter 7)* while his own daughters **'had grey beaver hats, then in fashion, shaded with ostrich plumes, and from under the brim of this graceful head-dress fell a profusion of light tresses, elaborately curled'** *(Volume 1, Chapter 7)*.

oppression using power to put other people down

The Reed family

Apart from Jane, the Reeds are the first characters that we get to know during the course of the novel. Jane's dislike of them is clear throughout, although she demonstrates how much she has changed by her treatment of them and her attitudes towards them when she returns to the house prior to Mrs Reed's death: 'I had once vowed that I would never call her aunt again: I thought it no sin to forget and break that vow, now' (Volume 2, Chapter 6).

Mrs Reed is described as strongly disliking Jane as a child, although it is not made clear why until later in the novel. She treats Jane very differently from how she treats her own children, and makes little secret of her dislike. On her deathbed, the reason for her dislike and the depth of her mistreatment of Jane is made clear.

In Volume 2, Chapter 6 she tells Jane that "I have twice done you a wrong which I regret now", but it is made clear that her regret is more for herself than for Jane: she notes that "Eternity is before me: I had better tell her", suggesting that the reason for her confession is for her own redemption and not for Jane's sake.

John is presented as an arrogant bully who treats Jane with contempt because of her social status. Described as a 'tyrant' at the start of the novel (Volume 1, Chapter 1), he becomes a gambler and is later described by his own mother as "sunk and degraded" (Volume 2, Chapter 6). However, she remains 'blind and deaf on the subject' (Volume 1, Chapter 1) of her son and refers to him as a "poor boy" (Volume 2, Chapter 6).

In Volume 1, Chapter 2 we learn **Georgiana** has a 'spoiled temper' and is 'universally indulged' as a child, whilst **Eliza** is 'head-strong and selfish'. In Georgiana's case, this leads her to become a vain adult who nonetheless makes an 'advantageous match with a wealthy worn-out man of fashion' who was willing to put up with her 'feeble-minded quailings' (Volume 2, Chapter 7). Eliza, on the other hand, becomes a nun who leaves her fortune to the nunnery.

> **Key quotations**
>
> [John's] look is frightful—I feel ashamed for him when I see him. *(Volume 2, Chapter 6)*
>
> "Georgiana, a more vain and absurd animal than you, was certainly never allowed to cumber the earth. You had no right to be born, for you make no use of life." *(Volume 2, Chapter 6)*

The Rivers family

The Rivers family are presented as the direct opposite of the Reed family: they are kind and generous in their dealings with Jane despite the fact that they are unaware of their family relationship.

Diana is described as a 'leader' whilst **Mary** is 'docile, intelligent, assiduous' *(Volume 3, Chapter 4)*. Both are employed as governesses and, much like Jane herself, are underappreciated for their skills and talents. They are both very close to their brother, but whilst they clearly admire him, they are not blind to his faults.

Both make good marriages: **'both Captain Fitzjames and Mr. Wharton love their wives, and are loved by them'** *(Volume 3, Conclusion),* which seems a just reward for their compassionate treatment of Jane.

Key quotations

There was a reviving pleasure in this intercourse, of a kind now tasted by me for the first time—the pleasure arising from perfect congeniality of tastes, sentiments, and principles. *(Volume 3, Chapter 4)*

It seemed I had found a brother: one I could be proud of,—one I could love; and two sisters, whose qualities were such, that when I knew them but as mere strangers, they had inspired me with genuine affection and admiration. *(Volume 3, Chapter 7)*

Activity 12

1. List some differences between the Rivers and Reed families. Add quotations to show how Brontë has used language to show Jane's feelings about each of the characters and families concerned.

2. Add further quotations from the text to support your ideas about Jane's feelings.

3. Now choose one Reed and one Rivers and write a paragraph in which you compare Jane's relationships with them. Remember to support your answer, and to comment specifically on how Brontë has used language to develop these ideas. Here is an example to help you:

It is obvious from the start of the novel that Jane's relationship with John Reed is a negative one: in her first description of him in Volume 1, Chapter 1, she describes him as inspiring 'terror'. Since he is only a child, this is shocking to the reader as it suggests that her feelings go beyond mere dislike to a fear of him and of what he might be capable of.

John Eyre

John Eyre is uncle to Jane and the Rivers siblings. He dies and leaves Jane a fortune of £20,000 which allows her the freedom to marry at the end of the novel. He is also responsible for the revelation about Rochester's intended bigamy following her letter to him prior to her wedding day.

Bertha Rochester (née Mason)

Bertha Rochester is the classic 'madwoman in the attic'. As a character, she appears infrequently and is barely described, but she is integral to the plot. Throughout most of the novel, she is confined to the attic like a caged animal, and her actions are characterized as animalistic and savage. The only descriptions of her come from Rochester, and therefore reflect his negative view of her.

She is powerless to affect change in her life until she eventually commits suicide by jumping from the roof of the burning house.

Bertha Rochester turns savage, as she has been trapped for so long.

Key quotations

"[...] I had marked neither modesty, nor benevolence, nor candour, nor refinement in her mind or manners—and, I married her [...]"
(Volume 3, Chapter 1)

"[...] I found her nature wholly alien to mine; her tastes obnoxious to me; her cast of mind common, low, narrow, and singularly incapable of being led to anything higher, expanded to anything larger [...]"
(Volume 3, Chapter 1)

As well as being a character in her own right, Bertha Mason represents the fear of that which was foreign and unknown. She also represents the oppression of women: she is confined to an attic because she was a passionate woman who lacked control. Her presence in the novel is a reminder that for a woman to be passionate was a dangerous thing.

Activity 13

It has been suggested that Bertha's role in the novel is more than a plot device. Taking each of these ideas in turn, can you find any evidence from the text to support them?

- She represents the attitude of the day about people from other cultures.
- She represents Victorian women who were generally powerless to do anything outside of the home.
- She represents what will happen to women who allow themselves to follow their passions rather than the expected codes of society.

Grace Poole

Grace Poole is the servant responsible for looking after Bertha Mason. At first Jane believes that Grace is the person who laughs insanely and sets Rochester's bed alight. It is Grace who warns Jane to lock her door at night. Jane assumes that Rochester's decision not to dismiss Grace is because she **'may possess originality and strength of character to compensate for the want of personal advantages'** *(Volume 2, Chapter 1)*. It is later revealed that she was hired from **'the Grimsby Retreat'** (an asylum) *(Volume 3, Chapter 1)* to look after Bertha. Her drunkenness is the eventual cause of Bertha's death, Thornfield's destruction and Rochester's injury.

Richard Mason

Rochester's former business partner from Jamaica, and Bertha's brother. On his first visit to Thornfield, he is bitten by her in spite of the fact that he shows concern for her welfare.

Mason arrives at the wedding in time to prevent Rochester from committing bigamy with Jane.

Miss Temple

Jane's first adult role model shows Jane what it is to be a good Christian. She treats the children in her care at Lowood with compassion, despite that being against the wishes of her employer, Mr Brocklehurst. She is an intelligent woman who understands when to act and when to be passive.

Key quotations

[...] **to her instruction I owed the best part of my acquirements; her friendship and society had been my continual solace; she had stood me in the stead of mother, governess, and, latterly, companion.**
(Volume 1, Chapter 10)

Miss Scatcherd

A teacher at Lowood who seems to take pleasure in making Helen's life miserable.

Mrs Fairfax

Her main role in the novel is as a plot device to fill in the gaps in Jane's knowledge. However, she also fulfils the role of a mother to Jane, advising her against falling in love with Rochester. A distant relative of Rochester, she misleads Jane about the laughter that she hears, letting her believe that it is Grace Poole that she can hear.

Mrs Fairfax shows a motherly concern for Jane

> **Key quotations**
>
> Mrs. Fairfax turned out to be what she appeared, a placid-tempered, kind-natured woman, of competent education and average intelligence. *(Volume 1, Chapter 12)*

Bessie Lee

Bessie is the only person from Jane's earliest years who shows her any affection. A servant, she tries to teach Jane how to make herself more acceptable to her aunt and cousins. Later, she visits Jane at Lowood.

Céline Varens

Adèle's mother and a woman with whom Rochester had an affair. He thought it was a **"grande passion"** *(Volume 1, Chapter 15)* but she was merely interested in his wealth. She claimed that Adèle was his daughter – something which he denies. She represents passion and the danger of women acting only upon their emotions and sexuality.

Adèle Varens

Adèle Varens is a young child throughout the course of the novel. She is the reason why Jane goes to work at Thornfield Hall, and usefully allows Brontë to reveal the view of the day in respect of both foreigners and Catholics. Jane is pleased to recount that **'a sound English education corrected in a great measure her French defects'** *(Volume 3, Conclusion)*, which also refers to a passionate nature.

> **Key quotations**
>
> [...] a superficiality of character, inherited probably from her mother, hardly congenial to an English mind. *(Volume 1, Chapter 15)*

Blanche Ingram

Although Blanche plays an important part in Jane's story in that she is Jane's rival for Rochester's affections, she is rather undeveloped as a character. She is merely a means for Rochester to test Jane's feelings for him and, once Jane has shown her love for him, Blanche is never mentioned again.

> **Key quotations**
>
> If he liked the majestic, she was the very type of majesty: then she was accomplished, sprightly. *(Volume 2, Chapter 2)*

Blanche is very much a **caricature** of a certain type of woman who would probably have been familiar to Brontë and who, it is very clear, she disliked. Even her name, which means 'pure', suggests that there is nothing much to her: she is a blank.

Activity 14

1. Look carefully at the extract below. What does it tell about Blanche as a character?

2. What does it reveal to us about Jane's attitude?

She was very showy, but she was not genuine: she had a fine person, many brilliant attainments; but her mind was poor, her heart barren by nature: nothing bloomed spontaneously on that soil; no unforced natural fruit delighted by its freshness. She was not good; she was not original: she used to repeat sounding phrases from books; she never offered, nor had, an opinion of her own. She advocated a high tone of sentiment; but she did not know the sensations of sympathy and pity: tenderness and truth were not in her. *(Volume 2, Chapter 3)*

Rosamond Oliver

Rosamond Oliver has all of the advantages that Jane lacks: she is wealthy, beautiful and generous. Despite this, and his obvious love of her, St. John chooses not to marry her because he knows that she would not make a good wife for a missionary. She acts as a **foil** to him, showing the extent to which his religious convictions have blinded him to other aspects of the world.

Jane's reliability as a narrator is called into question over her description of Miss Oliver whom she describes as **'not profoundly interesting'** *(Volume 3, Chapter 6)*.

> **caricature** a description in which certain features are exaggerated to make them appear ridiculous
>
> **foil** a character whose role is to highlight some aspect of another character's attitudes or beliefs

Activity 15

When we think about family, we often think about blood relationships. However, Jane is – or becomes part of – different families over the course of the novel.

Think about the relationships Jane forms in each of the four locations below. How close does she become to each character there? What does this show us? Some examples have been added to get you started.

- Gateshead – The Reed family: Jane related but on the outside **"you are less than a servant"** *(Volume 1, Chapter 2)*
- Lowood – Mr Brocklehurst: Jane part of the school but on the outside **"be on your guard against her"** *(Volume 1, Chapter 7)*
- Thornfield Hall
- Morton

Use quotations to support your ideas.

Writing about characters

Upgrade

In the novel, different characters represent different social groups that would have been familiar to Brontë. When it is relevant to the question, you should try to examine these different ideas to show that you understand not only the characters but also what Brontë was trying to show through her development of characters.

You should try to look at how the language that Brontë uses about the characters, as well as the language that she gives to the characters to use, reveals ideas about them and about society in the novel.

Character map

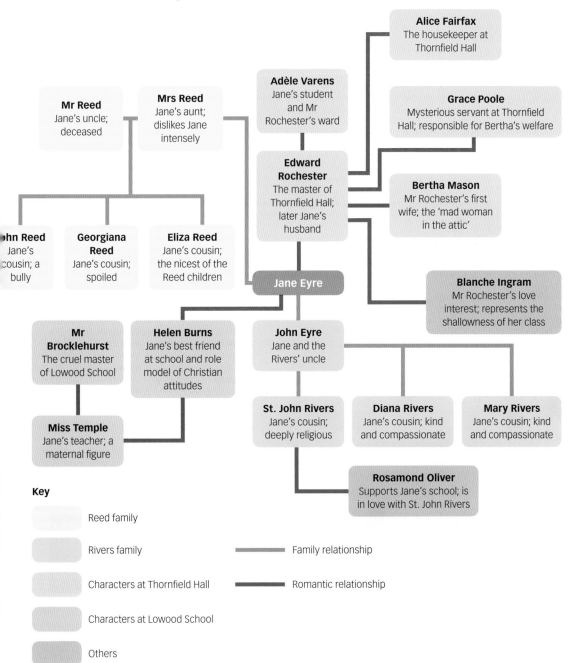

Alice Fairfax
The housekeeper at Thornfield Hall

Adèle Varens
Jane's student and Mr Rochester's ward

Grace Poole
Mysterious servant at Thornfield Hall; responsible for Bertha's welfare

Mr Reed
Jane's uncle; deceased

Mrs Reed
Jane's aunt; dislikes Jane intensely

Edward Rochester
The master of Thornfield Hall; later Jane's husband

Bertha Mason
Mr Rochester's first wife; the 'mad woman in the attic'

John Reed
Jane's cousin; a bully

Georgiana Reed
Jane's cousin; spoiled

Eliza Reed
Jane's cousin; the nicest of the Reed children

Jane Eyre

Blanche Ingram
Mr Rochester's love interest; represents the shallowness of her class

Mr Brocklehurst
The cruel master of Lowood School

Helen Burns
Jane's best friend at school and role model of Christian attitudes

John Eyre
Jane and the Rivers' uncle

Miss Temple
Jane's teacher; a maternal figure

St. John Rivers
Jane's cousin; deeply religious

Diana Rivers
Jane's cousin; kind and compassionate

Mary Rivers
Jane's cousin; kind and compassionate

Rosamond Oliver
Supports Jane's school; is in love with St. John Rivers

Key

Reed family

Rivers family

Characters at Thornfield Hall

Characters at Lowood School

Others

Family relationship

Romantic relationship

Brontë's use and choice of language is a crucial part of the novel's success. She uses vocabulary not just to tell the story, but to create strong **imagery** and to support the themes of the novel.

Narrative perspective

Jane Eyre is written as a fictional autobiography; therefore its **narrative perspective** is the first person 'I' throughout. This allows the reader to gain insight into the feelings of the narrator, but we are told in Volume 3, Conclusion that the autobiography was written ten years after Jane married Rochester and so the narrative is retrospective.

However, Brontë uses a variety of other narrative techniques to keep the reader alert.

Change in tense: Brontë sometimes heightens tension by making the narrator shift from the past tense to the present in order to impress on the reader the immediacy of the situation.

Use of third person: Occasionally Brontë, through the supposed narrator, distances the reader by having Jane refer to herself not in the first person but in the third person.

> **Key quotations**
>
> And yet, where was the Jane Eyre of yesterday?—where was her life?—where were her prospects?
>
> Jane Eyre, who had been an ardent, expectant woman—almost a bride—was a cold, solitary girl again [...] *(Volume 2, Chapter 11)*

In the quotation above, eerily the person, 'I', and the name 'Jane Eyre', seem to part company. Jane's return to Mr Rochester, having revealed her name to her relatives, the Rivers, is also an important reunion with self: "**I am Jane Eyre** [...] **I am come back to you**" *(Volume 3, Chapter 11)*. This use of language symbolically brings her journey of self-discovery and 'completion' as a character to its conclusion.

Tips for assessment

When you are writing about the language in the novel, it is important to think about *why* Brontë made the choices that she did.

complicit part of; an accomplice

imagery the use of visual or other vivid language to convey ideas or emotions

narrative perspective the position from which the story is told

Authorial voice: A further complication in the narrative perspective of the novel is when the author appears to interject, so that the reader gets Brontë's ideas rather than Jane's, or when the reader becomes unsure about whose point of view they are reading.

Brontë reminds the reader that they are reading something that has been constructed by making Jane address the reader directly at least 26 times during the course of the novel. This has the effect of distancing the reader, reminding them that they are reading a book and therefore making them reflect on what is going on rather than just following the story. This also intensifies the experience of reading the novel because it makes the reader **complicit** in Jane's point of view and makes them feel that they are in a special position of privilege in sharing the narrator's ideas and feelings.

Activity 1

1. One of the most famous instances of direct address in *Jane Eyre* is in the Conclusion: **'Reader, I married him.'** Look back through the novel and find the other occasions where we are addressed directly. Copy and complete the table below to explain the significance of each of these events:

Quotation	What or who it concerns	Significance
'Let the reader add, to complete the picture, refined features; a complexion, if pale, clear; and a stately air and carriage [...]' (Vol. 1, Ch. 5)	Miss Temple	Shows how deeply she admires her. Miss Temple is the first woman to treat Jane in a motherly way.
'True, reader; and I knew and felt this: and though I am a defective being, with many faults and few redeeming points, yet I never tired of Helen Burns [...]' (Vol. 1, Ch. 9)	Helen Burns	
'[...] in those days, reader, this now narrow catalogue of accomplishments, would have been held tolerably comprehensive.' (Vol. 1, Ch. 10)		

2. Why do you think that Brontë chose to have Jane speak directly to the reader? What do you think this contributes to the text?

   - Think about how the reader might feel being directly addressed.
   - Think about the relationship this creates between Jane and the reader.
   - Think about the overall effect this creates in the novel.

Images

Imagery is a key component in the mood of *Jane Eyre* and it is created through Brontë's careful choice of language. There are some images and words which recur frequently through the novel. It is no surprise that in pre-electric days a writer should comment on fires and candles, but these are mentioned so many times that they become a running thread, a **motif**.

Fire is a key motif throughout the novel

Fire

Both fire and candle are **proleptic**: they foreshadow events to come. These recurring motifs also carry other qualities. Fire is mentioned more than 80 times in the novel. Fire is a symbol of nurture – it keeps characters warm – but there is also a psychological significance when it is burning low or when it needs stoking. When Jane enters Rochester's parlour for the first time after returning to him, he is described as leaning over the fireplace where 'a neglected handful of fire burnt low in the grate' *(Volume 3, Chapter 11)*. The fire is clearly a metaphor for Rochester's subdued and reduced life; and is in direct contrast to the room Jane has just left where Rochester's manservant 'sat by a good fire'. The low fire also foreshadows Jane's description of Rochester's face later in the same chapter as 'a lamp quenched, waiting to be relit'.

Earlier in the novel the mention of fire in the various rooms all lead up to the moment when Bertha tries to set fire to Rochester's bed and then when she sets fire to Thornfield itself.

Fire also has an important link to the key theme of religion in the novel. The fires of hell are referred to when Brocklehurst questions Jane on where the wicked go after death: "And what is hell? Can you tell me that?" "A pit full of fire." *(Volume 1, Chapter 4)*, but Brontë also uses fire as an idea of rebirth. Through metaphorical 'trials of fire' Christians can **atone** for their sins and fire can therefore be seen as a cleansing tool. Rochester has literally suffered a trial of fire in the destruction of Thornfield, and the result of his injuries humbles him, leads to his repentance, and eventual 'resurrection'.

Tips for assessment

Upgrade

You will never be asked to write about an author's use of language in isolation. Be ready to reference other elements of the novel, such as any themes or relevant context to explain the effect of the author's language choices, and their wider implications. Add short, well-chosen quotations to demonstrate that you understand how all the elements of a novel link together.

Candles

In a similar way to fire, candles are an important motif, mentioned over 50 times. They are necessary to allow characters to move about in the dark, but they also allow characters to see – both literally and metaphorically.

Brontë also uses them as a subtle indication of social class and wealth. At Lowood Jane says **'we had only a short end of candle in our candlestick'** *(Volume 1, Chapter 10)*, which is in contrast to the blaze of light often described at Thornfield: **'[the] double illumination of fire and candle at first dazzled me'** *(Volume 1, Chapter 11)*.

Activity 2

Look at the references to fire and candles during Jane's time at Lowood. How does Brontë's choice of language reflect the conditions that Jane experiences there?

Brontë is more interested in building significance with repeated words and images than she is in symbolism, but there are some images which become **symbols**.

For example, when Jane is arguing with St. John, the motif of fire becomes a symbol of the contrast between their characters.

Key quotations

"And then," he pursued, "I am cold: no fervour infects me."

"Whereas I am hot, and fire dissolves ice. The blaze there has thawed all the snow from your cloak; by the same token, it has streamed on to my floor, and made it like a trampled street." *(Volume 3, Chapter 7)*

Activity 3

1. In the quotation above Jane describes herself as the 'fire' to St. John's ice. Find other examples in the text where Brontë has used the language of fire or heat to describe Jane's character.

2. What other repeated symbols does Brontë use in reference to Jane?

atone make amends

motif a word or phrase or image repeated during the course of the novel

proleptic forecasting the future; another word for foreshadowing

symbol a word which has a literal meaning but also another meaning of wider significance, representing an idea or concept

Symbolism

The red room

The red room is where Jane suffers a fit of terror when she is imprisoned there by Mrs Reed. She is left alone to face her own feelings and fears, despite calling out for help. In Volume 1, Chapter 3, Jane finds herself haunted by her **'frightful night-mare'** of **'a terrible red glare, crossed with thick black bars'**.

> **Key quotations**
>
> This room *<u>was chill</u>, because it seldom had a fire; it *<u>was silent</u>, because remote from the nursery and kitchens; *<u>solemn</u>, because it was known to be so seldom entered. *(Volume 1, Chapter 2)*
>
> *These three **clauses** use the same structure. This helps to emphasize the negative presentation of the room.

> **Activity 4**
>
> Read the next description of the red room from **'Daylight began to forsake'** to **'the embers of my decaying ire'** *(Volume 1, Chapter 2)*. How does Brontë use **figurative language** to enhance the negative mood in the red room?

Towards the end of the novel we learn of the attic room where Bertha is kept; the reader is reminded of the red room and therefore invited to make comparisons between Jane's childhood experiences and Bertha's adult one. The red room becomes a symbol of female imprisonment, both a literal one and a metaphorical one of being imprisoned within the confines of one's own mind.

A further potent symbol is the chestnut tree. Rochester proposes to Jane under the chestnut tree and it becomes a symbol of their relationship.

The splitting of the tree foreshadows Jane and Rochester's doomed wedding

> **Key quotations**
>
> [...] the great horse-chestnut at the bottom of the orchard had been struck by lightning in the night, and half of it split away.
> *(Volume 2, Chapter 8)*

The splitting of the tree is a foreshadowing of what will happen to Rochester. The tree itself becomes a symbol for Rochester. It is the first thing that Jane sees when she returns to Thornfield at the end of the novel and again seems to describe Rochester's current state.

[…] I faced the wreck of the chestnut tree; it stood up, black and riven: the trunk, split down the centre, gasped ghastly […] a ruin; but an entire ruin. *(Volume 2, Chapter 10)*

Books

Books and pictures are mentioned frequently in the novel. Books are a means of escape for Jane from the dreadful conditions both at Gateshead and Lowood. They are also a symbol for education and personal growth, as well as the world of the imagination. However, they can be less positive as St. John is seen retreating into his books at the end of the novel in order to avoid engaging with Jane. Perhaps by this stage of the novel Jane realizes that books, particularly the Bible and Hindustanee grammar, can be a vehicle for restriction rather than growth and development.

Names

Brontë places particular significance on the names of characters and places in *Jane Eyre*. Not all the names have symbolic values, but many of them do.

Character names

At first it is not clear that the name Reed has symbolic value, but when the word is used twice later on in the novel it brings to mind Jane's early experiences at Gateshead. In Volume 3, Chapter 1, Rochester says about Jane "never was anything at once so frail and so indomitable. A mere reed she feels in my hand!" At the end of the novel when Jane is at Moor House being persuaded to accept St. John's proposal, Jane describes herself like a reed: 'Oh, that gentleness! how far more potent is it than force! I could resist St. John's wrath: I grew pliant as a reed under his kindness' *(Volume 3, Chapter 9)*.

Ironically, Jane is more a reed than the Reeds themselves – they all snap under the pressures and troubles they face in life; only Jane bends and survives to live happy and content.

Other characters have names which symbolize their personal characteristics. The **onomatopoeic** Miss Scatcherd is a thorn in Helen's side. Miss Temple represents true Christian values at whose shrine many of the pupils worship. Grace is a positive virtue, but her love of alcohol is fatal. Mrs Fairfax is undoubtedly fair throughout.

clause a part of a sentence which makes sense on its own

figurative language words or expressions with a meaning that is different from the literal interpretation

onomatopoeia where the sound of the word suggests its meaning

St. John Rivers accrues several references to **John the Baptist** during the course of the novel, but his name asks the reader to reflect on whether his name attracts a certain irony, too.

Place names

The five houses which represent the five parts of *Jane Eyre* all have strong significance. Gateshead suggests the gates of Jane's origins. Lowood is situated in a low wood which breeds disease and kills off so many of its inmates. Thornfield reminds the reader of Jesus's crown of thorns: a curse and punishment which many of its inhabitants must endure. Moor House at Marsh End represents the solace which Jane finds after her wanderings in the wilderness. Ferndean is a wooded vale, perhaps reminding the reader of the biblical **vale of tears**.

Nature and the weather

It has been said that there is more weather in *Jane Eyre* than in almost any other English novel. Nearly every outdoor scene has a description of the landscape and the weather and many of the indoor scenes also refer to the weather. Brontë establishes and alters the mood and atmosphere of her scenes by using natural descriptions in a rather similar way to how she uses the presence and/or absence of fires and candles to create the mood and atmosphere of indoor scenes.

The beginning of Chapter 6, for example, parallels the harshness of the regime at Lowood with the weather conditions.

> **Key quotations**
>
> The next day commenced as before, getting up and dressing by rushlight; but this morning we were obliged to dispense with the ceremony of washing: the water in the pitchers was frozen. A change had taken place in the weather the preceding evening, and a keen north-east wind, whistling through the crevices of our bedroom windows all night long, had made us shiver in our beds, and turned the contents of the ewers to ice. *(Volume 1, Chapter 6)*

Activity 5

Read the extract in Volume 1, Chapter 5 that begins 'The garden was a wide enclosure' to 'the sound of a hollow cough'. Explain how Brontë uses the weather in this extract to reflect Jane's emotions, set the mood and predict future events.

Support your ideas with key words or phrases from the extract.

John the Baptist a distinctive and fearless preacher in the time of Jesus, who believed unfailingly in his religious mission. He was beheaded by Herod Antipas

vale of tears the trials of life Christians leave behind when they enter Heaven

Jane's arrival at Ferndean is preceded by an extended description of the landscape which sets the mood and atmosphere for her meeting with Rochester.

> **Key quotations**
>
> There was a grass-grown track descending the forest-aisle, between hoar and knotty shafts and under branched arches. I followed it [...] The darkness of natural as well as of sylvan dusk, gathered over me! I looked round in search of another road. There was none: all was interwoven stem, columnar trunk, dense, summer foliage—no opening anywhere. *(Volume 3, Chapter 11)*

Pathetic fallacy

Sometimes the description of nature and the weather is extended by Brontë into pathetic fallacy where the elements of nature and the weather become a metaphorical way of describing the thoughts and feelings of a character.

A good example of the use of pathetic fallacy is the night before Jane's wedding. Outside, she observes the moon.

> **Key quotations**
>
> The wind represents how Jane feels.
>
> The moon is half in shadow – suggesting a shadow has been cast over Jane's wedding day.
>
> This is the wind, but also Bertha, yet Jane has no understanding of what is going on.
>
> [...] I ran before the wind [...] the moon appeared momentarily in that part of the sky which filled their fissure; her disc was blood-red and half overcast; she seemed to throw on me one bewildered, dreary glance, and buried herself again instantly in the deep drift of cloud. The wind fell, for a second, round Thornfield; but far away over wood and water poured a wild, melancholy wail: it was sad to listen to, and I ran off again. *(Volume 2, Chapter 10)*
>
> Reminds us of the red room, of Bertha's attack on Mason and the lifeblood of Jane herself.
>
> The moon becomes clouded over just as Jane's thoughts are clouded.
>
> Thorns symbolize suffering and sacrifice – Jesus's crown of thorns.
>
> Jane is sad, without understanding why.

The red moon before her wedding day reflects Jane's unease

The gothic

Brontë draws on the gothic tradition for those elements of the novel which involve the supernatural, the wild picturesque landscapes and especially the mystery of the madwoman in the attic. There are moments when Rochester sees Jane as fairy-like and when Jane first arrives at Thornfield she says **'I thought I caught a glimpse of a fairy place'** *(Volume 1, Chapter 11)*, perhaps ironically foreshadowing the gothic element of Bertha, the madwoman in the attic.

The atmosphere at Gateshead, too, has a gothic quality to it, described as Jane looks in the mirror.

Everything about the attic where Bertha is kept at Thornfield has a gothic quality: **'the attic seemed black as a vault [...] like a corridor in some Bluebeard's castle'** *(Volume 1, Chapter 11)*. Bertha herself appears to Jane to be like a phantom even before she knows who she is: **'I started wide awake on hearing a vague murmur, peculiar and lugubrious'** *(Volume 1, Chapter 15)*. Mason describes Bertha as a vampire: **"She sucked the blood: she said she'd drain my heart"** *(Volume 2, Chapter 5)*.

When Jane describes her dream to Rochester, she does so very much in gothic terms. This description clearly foreshadows the terrible fate that will befall Thornfield Hall.

> **Key quotations**
>
> **"I dreamt another dream, sir: that Thornfield Hall was a dreary ruin, the retreat of bats and owls [...] I wandered, on a moonlight night, through the grass-grown enclosure within: here I stumbled over a marble hearth, and there over a fallen fragment of cornice."** *(Volume 2, Chapter 10)*

The cry from Rochester in Volume 3, Chapter 9 that Jane supernaturally and psychically hears and which draws her to him is another gothic element in the novel.

> **Activity 6**
>
> Look at the visits that Jane receives from Bertha Rochester during the night:
>
> Volume 1, Chapter 15 from **'Just then it seemed my chamber-door was touched'** to **'all was still'**.
>
> Volume 2, Chapter 10 from **"All the preface, sir; the tale is yet to come"** to **"I became insensible from terror"**.
>
> What gothic elements has Brontë used in these episodes, and what are their effects?

Irony

A further language technique used by Brontë is irony, where the character does not appreciate the full significance of what he or she says. It is used predominantly in the middle of the novel, particularly surrounding events of the wedding. In the playful interchange between Rochester, Jane and Adèle in Volume 2, Chapter 9 Adèle says to Rochester about Jane **"She will have nothing to eat: you will starve her"**. After Rochester's deceit and the failed marriage, Jane is on the road and literally starving.

Later in the same chapter Jane says light-heartedly to Rochester **"I'll be preparing myself to go out as a missionary to preach liberty to them that are enslaved"** *(Volume 2, Chapter 9)*. She is completely unaware of what will happen with St. John. In Volume 2, Chapter 10 when faced with her calling cards Jane says **'Mrs Rochester! She did not exist'**. Jane does not know what will happen on her wedding day and is, as yet, unaware of Bertha's existence.

Rochester's future too is ironically prophesied as he says to Jane **"Is Thornfield Hall a ruin? Am I severed from you by insuperable obstacles?"** *(Volume 2, Chapter 10)*. Rochester is unaware of the impending fire, the severing of his arm and the severing of relations between himself and Jane. On her way to the wedding Jane says **'I know not whether the day was fair or foul'** *(Volume 2, Chapter 11),* unaware of what will happen and oblivious to the evil which surrounds the witches in *Macbeth* from whom the quotation is taken.

Writing about language

Upgrade

Remember, an author's language choices are a crucial part of the way the text has been crafted. Examiners are often disappointed that students do not write in enough detail about an author's use of language, particularly when they are asked to comment on an extract from the novel.

Include reference to the following areas:

- Brontë's choice of narrative voice and how this helps involve the reader in Jane's story

- how motifs are used for effect and build in importance throughout the text

- the ways Brontë uses symbols to signal to the reader

- how characters are created more vividly through symbolism

- how Brontë crafts mood using the weather

- the gothic influence on the novel

- the use of irony to foreshadow future events.

Themes

This novel explores several different themes, many of which interlink. In the exam, you may be asked to write about one of these themes, so you need to ensure that you are familiar with them, and with how they are developed.

The position of women

Charlotte Brontë would have been well aware of the difficulty of being a woman in the 19th century. As the daughter of a clergyman, she would have had a good social standing, but a small dowry, which would not have made her a good prospect as a wife. This is similar to the position that Jane finds herself in in the novel.

As a single woman, Jane has little power over her own life. Her only option for employment is to work as a governess; a job which offers little security. With no money of her own, no relatives to care for her, and no prospect of marriage, she would have had little choice but to remain a governess all of her life. As a childless single woman, she would have been greatly pitied, since motherhood was considered a significant part of the role of a woman.

At the time of the novel, it was commonly thought that women and men should exist in what were known as 'separate spheres' with women being considered to be more moral than men, but less physically able. Since women were largely confined to working in the home, this was even considered a reason not to give them the vote.

Victorian society had very clear expectations of what an 'ideal' middle-class woman was like. She should:

- be married and have children
- spend her time in the home
- sing and play a musical instrument
- speak a little French or Italian
- be involved in **philanthropic** work
- be ignorant of intellectual topics, leaving those to her husband
- be largely reliant on her husband.

An idealistic Victorian family scene

philanthropic charitable work, such as teaching in Sunday school. This work was often linked to religious organizations

Activity 1

1. Is Jane Eyre an 'ideal' Victorian woman? Consider each of the seven expectations of the ideal Victorian woman in turn, and make a note of which of them she meets. Give quotations from the text to support your answer.

2. Now think about the female characters listed below. How 'ideal' are they, according to the expectations on page 78?

- The Reed sisters
- The Rivers sisters
- Blanche Ingram
- Rosamond Oliver
- Bertha Mason

While some of the women in the novel clearly accept their social position, Jane refuses to do so. Her suggestion in Volume 1, Chapter 12 that 'Women are supposed to be very calm generally: but women feel just as men feel; they need exercise for their faculties, and a field for their efforts as much as their brothers do; they suffer from too rigid a restraint, too absolute a stagnation, precisely as men would suffer; and it is narrow-minded in their more privileged fellow-creatures to say that they ought to confine themselves to making puddings and knitting stockings, to playing on the piano and embroidering bags' was considered shocking by readers at the time. St. John Rivers is shocked: 'He had not imagined that a woman would dare to speak so to a man. For me, I felt at home in this sort of discourse' *(Volume 3, Chapter 6)*.

Activity 2

In 1792, Mary Wollstonecraft wrote in her book *A Vindication of the Rights of Women*:

> I hope my own sex will excuse me if I treat them like rational creatures, instead of flattering their fascinating graces and viewing them as if they were in a state of perpetual childhood and unable to stand alone.

Considering this quotation, to what extent are women in the novel presented as being 'in a state of perpetual childhood and unable to stand alone'?

- Choose three or four of the female characters, including Jane, and make a list of the ways in which they are presented in this way, as well as examples where they are not.

- Now turn this into a timeline across the novel for each of your chosen characters, thinking about how they change, if applicable, across the story, and the reasons for those changes.

- Next, turn these ideas into paragraphs, supporting your ideas with evidence from the text.

Tips for assessment

Remember that you can improve your answer by making links between the themes of the novel and the context. Make sure that your answer shows that you have thought about why Brontë might have presented her female characters in this way: think about what impact she might have wanted to have on her readers.

Social class

For a modern reader, the issue of social class may not be as clear cut as it would have been to the reader at the time. It would have been uncommon for people to move out of the class into which they were born, and friendships – and certainly relationships – across class boundaries would have been unusual. As Mrs Fairfax notes: "Gentlemen in his station are not accustomed to marry their governesses" *(Volume 2, Chapter 9)*.

As a governess, Jane is effectively between classes. She is not a member of the upper classes for whom she works, but neither is she a member of the lower class. This allows her to interact with members of all classes and Brontë to shine a light on the attitudes of the different classes.

Activity 3

1. The quotations which follow reveal something of the attitudes to class in the novel. The first quotation has been analysed for you as an example; copy out and annotate the others to explain what attitudes to class are presented.

Because Jane is an orphan, she is reliant on the Reeds for her home and her upkeep.

Suggesting that Jane should behave like a pauper who would be far below John in class.

"You have no business to take our books: you are a dependant [...] you ought to beg, and not to live here with gentlemen's children like us, and eat the same meals we do, and wear clothes at our mama's expense." *(Volume 1, Chapter 1)*

Juxtaposes the upper class "gentlemen's children" with Jane's status, showing how low John thinks she is.

The collective pronoun 'we' contrasts with 'you' showing how different John considers Jane to be.

"[...] I anticipated only coldness and stiffness: this is not like what I have heard of the treatment of governesses; but I must not exult too soon." *(Volume 1, Chapter 11)*

"[...] they are only servants, and one can't converse with them on terms of equality: one must keep them at due distance, for fear of losing one's authority." *(Volume 1, Chapter 11)*

2. Now find more quotations from different places in the text which also reveal ideas about social class. Annotate them as you have done here.

Despite her own uncertain position, Jane shares the prevailing attitudes of the day regarding the poor. Her attitude to her new life as the mistress of Morton School reveals that she feels superior to the children that she is responsible for.

Key quotations

This morning, the village school opened. I had twenty scholars. But three of the number can read: none write or cypher. [...] They speak with the broadest accent of the district. At present, they and I have a difficulty in understanding each other's language. Some of them are unmannered, rough, intractable, as well as ignorant; but others are docile, have a wish to learn, and evince a disposition that pleases me. I must not forget that these coarsely-clad little peasants are of flesh and blood as good as the scions of gentlest genealogy; and that the germs of native excellence, refinement, intelligence, kind feeling, are as likely to exist in their hearts as in those of the best-born. [...] I was weakly dismayed at the ignorance, the poverty, the coarseness of all I heard and saw round me.
(Volume 3, Chapter 5)

Activity 4

Look carefully at the key quotation above, and then answer the following questions:

- Jane's thoughts about the children at Morton School are mixed: she expresses both negative and hopeful feelings towards them. Make a list of the reasons that she gives for each of these feelings.

- What evidence is there to suggest that Jane considers herself superior to the children at Morton School?

- What evidence is there to suggest that she feels that she has a moral obligation to help them?

- Now draw all of these ideas together to answer the question below. Make sure that you give clear evidence to support your answer.

> What does the extract suggest about Brontë's attitude to differences in class? How does Brontë present the idea in this extract and elsewhere in the novel?

The Victorian period was a period of great change, and many people found it difficult to balance their desire to better themselves with the social conventions of their time. Jane demonstrates that it was possible to make good marriages, but it is clear that Jane's difficult start in life is, at least in part, due to her mother's choice to marry 'beneath her' *(Volume 1, Chapter 3)*.

Due to the way in which society worked, a woman's class was always based on the roles of her husband: as a clergyman's wife, Mrs Eyre's status is lower than that of her sister, who marries well. As a dependant, Jane's status is lower still.

Another important aspect of class in the novel is that of foreignness. There are a number of characters in the novel who are foreign, and the attitudes of the English characters towards them is striking.

Modern attitudes to race are very different but, in the Victorian period, it was considered a moral duty to 'improve' other foreign races by exposing them to English values and ideas. In many cases, this was done by religious figures, such as St. John Rivers, undertaking missionary work.

Religion

A major theme of the novel is religion, with different characters representing different religious attitudes. At the time of the novel, religion was a very important part of society and people were very open about their religious beliefs. However, it was also a time of great change in religious attitudes, which is perhaps why this is such a prominent theme in the novel.

Activity 5

None of the three views of religion presented by the characters of Mr Brocklehurst, Helen Burns or St. John Rivers are, in the end, shown to be entirely satisfactory.

1. With a partner, discuss how these views of religion are shown to be less than satisfactory. Think about:
   - what the characters gain from their religious convictions
   - what the characters lose from their religious convictions.

2. What do you think Brontë's views about religious belief are, based on the ideas that she has presented in the novel? Give evidence to support your ideas.

3. Consider the approaches to religion which Jane encounters throughout the novel. What conclusion do you think Brontë wanted her reader to come to about religion? Why?

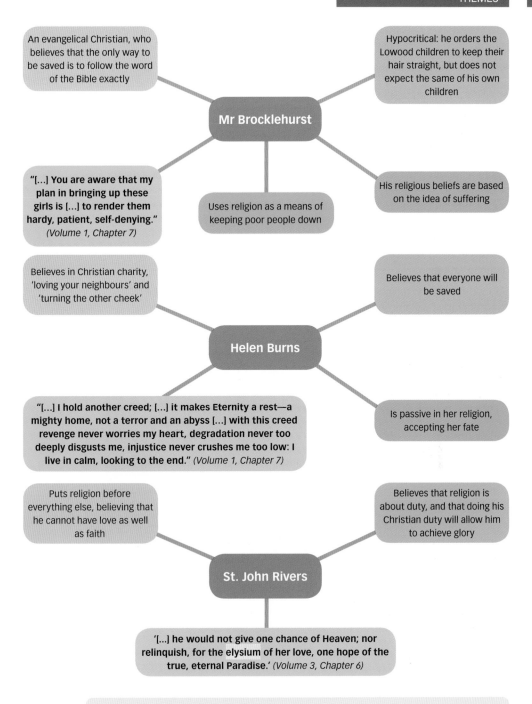

An evangelical Christian, who believes that the only way to be saved is to follow the word of the Bible exactly

Hypocritical: he orders the Lowood children to keep their hair straight, but does not expect the same of his own children

Mr Brocklehurst

"[...] You are aware that my plan in bringing up these girls is [...] to render them hardy, patient, self-denying." *(Volume 1, Chapter 7)*

Uses religion as a means of keeping poor people down

His religious beliefs are based on the idea of suffering

Believes in Christian charity, 'loving your neighbours' and 'turning the other cheek'

Believes that everyone will be saved

Helen Burns

"[...] I hold another creed; [...] it makes Eternity a rest—a mighty home, not a terror and an abyss [...] with this creed revenge never worries my heart, degradation never too deeply disgusts me, injustice never crushes me too low: I live in calm, looking to the end." *(Volume 1, Chapter 7)*

Is passive in her religion, accepting her fate

Puts religion before everything else, believing that he cannot have love as well as faith

Believes that religion is about duty, and that doing his Christian duty will allow him to achieve glory

St. John Rivers

'[...] he would not give one chance of Heaven; nor relinquish, for the elysium of her love, one hope of the true, eternal Paradise.' *(Volume 3, Chapter 6)*

elysium the dwelling place of the blessed after death in Greek mythology; a place of perfect bliss

As a clergyman's daughter herself, Brontë would have been very aware of the central **tenets** of the Christian faith, which include:

- justification by faith: the idea that belief in God leads to a relationship with God
- life after death
- redemption: the idea that there is a price to be paid in order to be freed from the consequences of sin.

It is clear from the novel that these tenets influenced her writing and her portrayal of religion in the novel. Of all of the characters, Rochester is perhaps the one for whom religious beliefs are the most important to his story. Although not a man of God like St. John Rivers, the development of his faith ultimately leads to the satisfactory conclusion to his story. He tells Jane that "of late—I began to see and acknowledge the hand of God in my doom. I began to experience remorse, repentance; the wish for reconcilement to my Maker" *(Volume 3, Chapter 11)*. It is this true repentance and faith that Brontë ultimately rewards, allowing him to be reunited with Jane.

His journey through religious faith is an interesting one, in that he is not a conventionally religious character, unlike Helen Burns and St. John Rivers.

Activity 6

1. Look at the list of ideas and quotations below relating to Rochester. Categorize them into those which show traditional Christian values and ideas of the time, and those which do not.

> "[Céline Varens] had two successors" *(Volume 3, Chapter 1)*

> "See that she is cared for as her condition demands, and you have done all that God and humanity require of you." *(Volume 3, Chapter 1)*

> Rochester's proposal to Jane

> "I did wrong: I would have sullied my innocent flower—breathed guilt on its purity: the Omnipotent snatched it from me." *(Volume 3, Chapter 11)*

> Rochester's marriage to Bertha Mason

> Rochester takes responsibility for Adèle

2. Considering everything we know about Rochester, do you believe that it is right that 'God had tempered judgment with mercy' *(Volume 3, Conclusion)* at the end of the novel? Explain why, with close reference to the text.

tenet firm belief or principle

While St. John and Brocklehurst live their religious lives publicly, both Jane and Rochester practise their religion in a much more private manner. As a child, Jane's view of religion was rather unconventional.

Key quotations

"Do you know where the wicked go after death?"

"They go to hell," was my ready and orthodox answer.

"And what is hell? Can you tell me that?"

"A pit full of fire."

"And should you like to fall into that pit and to be burning there for ever?"

"No, sir."

"What must you do to avoid it?"

I deliberated a moment; my answer when it did come, was objectionable: "I must keep in good health, and not die."

(Volume 1, Chapter 4)

John Calvin (1509–1564) established Calvinism, which is a branch of Protestantism that states that people are fundamentally immoral

It is clear from the extract above that the young Jane understands the concept of life after death, but that her view is not in accord with Brocklehurst's Calvinist perspective. Rather like Rochester, Jane's religious beliefs and understanding develop over the course of the novel and, although she rejects all of the models of religion that other characters show, she develops her own Christian faith based on the lessons that she learns from others.

 Activity 7

Create a timeline for Jane's religious development, thinking about the different influences on her beliefs, and the ways in which they affect her beliefs and actions.

Human desire vs. social conventions

Within the novel, there is clear focus on the issue of the clash between following one's human desires and following the conventions of society. From the outset, Jane struggles to conform to what society expects of her, and it is this struggle which is at the heart of the novel. This struggle manifests itself in several different ways during the course of the novel.

As a child, Jane rebels against society's expectations of her, both as a girl and as a dependant.

Activity 8

Look again at Chapters 1 to 4 of Volume 1.

1. Make a list of the ways in which Jane refuses to conform to the expectations of a child who is:

   - female
   - a dependant.

2. For each item in your list, add a quotation from the text to support your point.

3. Discuss your choices with a partner. What do each of these things suggest to the reader about Jane's attitude to the world?

Later in the novel, it is not her status that is a possible cause for rebellion but her moral obligations. She cannot stay with Rochester because he is married, so she leaves Thornfield Hall; on this occasion, she acts as would have been socially acceptable at the time. This suggests a change in her attitude: rather than following her heart, as she would have done in the past, she follows her head.

Activity 9

Jane states that **'Laws and principles are not for the times when there is no temptation: they are for such moments as this, when body and soul rise in mutiny against their rigour'** *(Volume 3, Chapter 1)*.

Look again at the extract in Volume 3, Chapter 1 which begins **"Mr. Rochester, I will *not* be yours"** and ends **"Farewell, for ever!"** With a partner, discuss the extract and make notes on how Brontë presents Jane's struggle between her human desires and the conventions of society.

Jane is not the only character who struggles to find a path between following her desires and behaving in a socially acceptable manner. Although this is more often an issue for the female characters, who are more constrained by their gender and class than the male characters, it is possible to see that many of the characters experience such struggles in the novel.

When Jane tells Miss Temple about her childhood, Brontë describes how Jane **'resolved in the depth of my heart that I would be most moderate [...] I infused into the narrative far less of gall and wormwood than ordinary. Thus restrained and simplified, it sounded more credible'** *(Volume 1, Chapter 8)*. This shows that Jane understands, thanks to Helen Burns, the importance of keeping her natural desire for passion and passionate expression under control: this element of restraint in her character helps her to become more satisfied with her life.

Activity 10

1. Copy and complete the table below to show which characters experience personal struggles within the novel, and why. Give evidence from the text to support your answers.

Character	What struggle does this character face?	Reason	Evidence from the text
Rochester	commitment to his marriage vs desire to escape from it	religion	
St. John Rivers			
Bertha Mason			

2. With a partner, discuss which of the characters undergoes the greatest struggle and why. Which of the characters undergoes the least struggle? Why? Link your ideas closely to evidence from the text.

Love and marriage

Familial love

One of the most striking aspects of Jane's relationships within the novel is that she experiences no **familial** love. As a child, she is orphaned and spends her early years with an aunt and cousins who actively dislike her, so her first clear experience of familial love is at the hands of Miss Temple when she goes to school.

However, when we look at the novel as a whole, it becomes clear that there are many characters in the novel who have relationships with Jane which could be considered to be loving, for example: Bessie, Helen Burns, Miss Temple, Adèle, Mrs Fairfax, Diana and Mary St. John, and of course Mr Rochester.

Romantic love

The novel presents two contrasting views of marriage: the marriage of convenience and marriage based on mutual love.

Rochester's first marriage, to Bertha Mason, is for financial reasons. In Volume 3, Chapter 1, he describes how he **"must be provided for by a wealthy marriage"** and his father found him a bride who would bring a **"fortune of thirty-thousand pounds"** to the marriage. While a modern reader might find this attitude surprising, and possibly even unacceptable, this attitude was very common at the time of the novel.

familial relating to family

Activity 11

Marriages of convenience worked both ways with women and men both gaining from them.

- Discuss with a partner the reasons why marriages of convenience might have been effective.
- Now think about how each of these ideas is reflected in the novel. Use quotations to support your points.

Rochester reveals to Jane that, in his marriage to Bertha, **"I never loved, I never esteemed, I did not even know her"** *(Volume 3, Chapter 1)*. Jane's marriage to him, in contrast, is based on mutual love: **'Not a human being that ever lived could wish to be loved better than I was loved; and him who thus loved me I absolutely worshipped'** *(Volume 3, Chapter 1)*. In this way, Brontë presents marriages based on love as being more satisfying than those based on convenience.

Jane and Rochester marry for love, rather than for financial reasons

Although Jane and Rochester marry for love, it is important to remember that, significantly, this does not happen until after Jane has received her inheritance.

As well as the two marriages which take place (or have taken place) in the novel, there are also a number of marriages that do not happen: those of Rochester and Blanche, Jane and St. John and St. John and Rosamond. In each case, there are clear reasons for these marriages not going ahead despite the fact that they would make acceptable unions.

Activity 12

1. For each of the potential marriages mentioned above, discuss with a partner what the advantages of each would be, as well as why they ultimately don't happen.

2. Thinking about all of the marriages mentioned in the novel, what views do you think Charlotte Brontë has about marriage? Support your ideas with evidence from the text.

3. At the end of the novel, Jane is married. Some readers feel that this is an unsatisfactory ending, because Jane has failed to achieve the independence that she wanted. To what extent do you agree that Jane's marriage at the end of the novel is an unsatisfactory conclusion?

Think about:

- what she gains by being married
- what she loses by being married
- what a reader now might think, and why
- what a reader at the time would have thought, and why.

Search for identity

As a Bildungsroman, the whole novel focuses on Jane's growing up and her search for her own identity. She is the orphaned daughter of a clergyman, a dependant, a governess and, finally, a wife and mother. However, she strives to be seen as a person in her own right, often defying the expectations of Victorian society to do so.

Identity is often linked with other themes within the novel; social class, gender and religion all play a part in how Jane sees herself and how others see her.

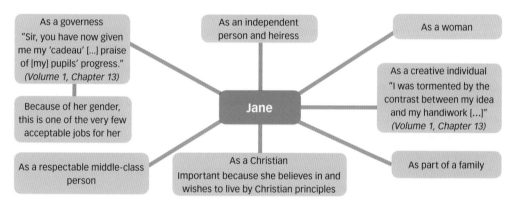

As a governess
"Sir, you have now given me my 'cadeau' [...] praise of [my] pupils' progress."
(Volume 1, Chapter 13)

As an independent person and heiress

As a woman

As a creative individual
"I was tormented by the contrast between my idea and my handiwork [...]"
(Volume 1, Chapter 13)

Because of her gender, this is one of the very few acceptable jobs for her

Jane

As a respectable middle-class person

As a Christian
Important because she believes in and wishes to live by Christian principles

As part of a family

Although the novel focuses on Jane, the theme of identity is not confined to the female characters. Although men in this period may have had more defined roles, both Rochester and St. John Rivers are at times, searching for their own identity.

Activity 13

1. Copy and complete the diagram above to show the different elements of Jane's identity. Use quotations from the text to develop the diagram. For each of the themes, write down why they are important to Jane's identity. One has been done for you as an example.

2. Now think about Jane's identity as a whole. Which elements of her identity make her happiest? Explain why with close reference to the text.

3. Using the diagram about Jane's identity as a model, complete one for Rochester and one for St. John Rivers. In each case, consider why they are searching to find their place in society.

Writing about themes in the novel

Upgrade

When you write about a theme, it is important to be clear about how it develops across the novel as a whole. You will need to consider *why* Brontë might have presented the theme in the way that she did.

Even if the question that you are asked is not specifically about a theme, you will still need to show that you have understood themes. For example, if you are writing about the character of St. John Rivers, you will need to be able to show how religion is an essential part of his character, and therefore his behaviour.

Exam skills

Understanding the question

Before you begin your assessment, read the questions carefully. You may have a choice of questions, there may only be one question or there may be one question in two parts. If the question is in parts, look at the number of marks awarded to each part. Then divide the time you have available for the answer in proportion to the marks. For example, if you have 45 minutes to answer a two-part question where part a) is worth 20 marks and part b) is worth 20 marks, it is clear that you should spend around 20 minutes on each part, allowing five minutes in total for planning.

You may be given an extract from the novel in the exam and be asked to use it in your answer, as well as referring to the rest of the novel. If this is the case, you will be expected to refer in detail to the extract, quoting where appropriate. You should be selective in how you use the rest of the novel, making sure that your chosen references and quotations are relevant to the question.

Try to approach the question methodically. Start by identifying what the question is actually asking you to do: you could underline the key words and phrases, and note down what they mean. Exam questions include certain words and phrases that are used quite often. Learn what they mean and they will tell you what you need to write about.

Explore means look at all the different aspects of something. For example, 'Explore how the author presents Jane' means you need to look at the author's presentation of Jane's character when she is with different people such as Mrs Reed and Helen Burns. You also need to look at how and why Jane's character might be presented differently in those situations, as well as the way in which the writer describes her when she is presented on her own.

How does the author... or *show how...* means explain the techniques the author uses to create a specific effect. For example, 'How does Brontë present ideas about class in this extract?' means you need to look at how the author shows attitudes to people of different class in the extract. Think about the language used and pick out details such as dialogue and description. Look also at how different characters behave in relation to one another.

Present and *portray* are similar words for looking at a character and prompt you to consider not only what the character is like, but also what devices the author uses to show this. For example, 'How is Jane presented/portrayed?' means you need to say how she is described; what Brontë makes her say and do, and why; how Brontë shows other characters reacting to her; and how the author shows her changing over the course of the novel.

In what ways... means look at different sides of something. For example, 'In what ways is Helen Burns significant?' means you need to look at more than just the fact that she is Jane's first real friend. You need to explain what Helen's attitude to life is; how and why different characters respond to her in different ways; why Brontë presents her death in the way that she does; and whether her impact goes beyond the chapters in which she appears.

What role... means write not just about the character and how they are shown but also about their function in the novel. For example, 'What role does St. John Rivers play?' means you need to write about his character and how it is shown, but also about why he is in the novel at all. You could try imagining the novel without him. He saves Jane from death, allowing the novel to continue, but he also shows a side to religion and religious belief that Jane does not share. He asks her to marry him, but his reasoning for doing so is not based on love. The final words of the novel are about him.

Explain or *comment on* are phrases that invite you to give your response to something in as much detail as you can. For example, 'Explain the importance of independence in the novel' means you should write about who has independence in the novel and who doesn't. You will also need to write about why some characters have more independence than others and what impact that has on their actions in the novel.

How far... means you need to evaluate the extent of something. For example, in response to 'How far do you agree that religion is at the heart of the novel?' you should write about religion but also consider other themes that are important to the novel, such as ideas about love and social class. You need to make sure that you consider a range of ideas but come back to the original question and say whether you agree or disagree that it is 'central'.

Examining the question

Look at the question below. The key words and phrases have been highlighted and explained.

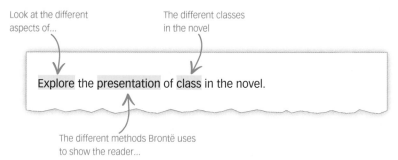

Look at the different aspects of...

The different classes in the novel

Explore the presentation of class in the novel.

The different methods Brontë uses to show the reader...

You are being asked to do a number of things in this question. You need to look at:

- how Brontë presents the upper classes
- how Brontë presents the lower classes
- how she shows the classes interacting with one another
- what the relationship between the classes shows about society at the time.

Activity 1

1. Write out the following question:

   > Show how Helen Burns is important to the novel as a whole.

   a) Highlight or underline the key words and phrases. Then describe what you are being asked to do.

   b) Make a list of things you need to do to answer the question.

2. With a partner, imagine you are the Chief Examiner.

   a) Write two or three questions that you think might appear in this part of the exam. Try to word them as they would be written on an actual paper. Check your exam board's website to find example questions.

   b) Swap with another pair and analyse each other's questions as in question 1.

Planning your answer

It is worth taking five minutes to plan your answer before you start to write it. Plan an effective structure for your answer and add pointers for the information you need to include in each section. Then when you write the actual answer, you will be free to concentrate on your writing style and to make sure you have used the correct terminology and included evidence to support your points.

Candidates who use their own ideas about the text produce fresher and more interesting answers than candidates who have prepared possible answers to almost every question in advance. So the key is to practise planning answers to a variety of questions but, if you want to write practice answers, don't learn them by heart!

Below are several different ways of planning an essay. Any of these methods would help you to gather ideas for your answer and set out the information you need to include clearly.

Lists

You can list points that you want to include, perhaps with a brief note of the evidence you will use. Remember you need to ensure that each point focuses on the question. You could do this by arranging your list in two columns. This is what the beginning of a two-column list might look like for the following question:

> Explore the presentation of Rochester in the novel.

Technique (presentation)	Effects (what it tells us about Rochester)
Intro – introduced to the reader without a name; described as having 'dark' features (Volume 1, Chapter 12).	Suggests he is mysterious and possibly dangerous.
How do other people respond to him (Mrs Fairfax, Adèle, Jane)? Mrs F. sees him as 'nothing more' than her employer (Volume 1, Chapter 11).	Insignificant to Mrs F. on a personal level – he is just her boss. Suggests that he keeps himself distant.

Activity 2

1. Create a two-column plan for each of the following questions:

   a) To what extent do you think that religion and religious views are central to the novel?

   b) What role do dreams and visions play in the novel as a whole?

   c) Explain the importance of social class in the novel.

2. In pairs or small groups, compare the plans you have created. Exchange ideas and add to and amend your plans as necessary. Add a star next to what you consider to be the most important points in each plan. Be prepared to share your ideas with the class.

Spider diagrams

You could also use a spider diagram to plan your answer. You need to ensure that your plan remains focused on the key words of the question: 'Explore' (i.e. look at the different aspects), 'presentation' (i.e. the techniques Brontë uses) and 'Rochester'.

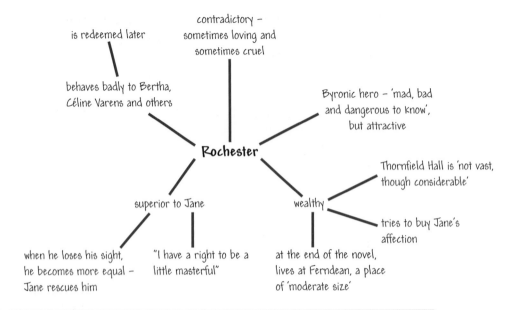

is redeemed later

contradictory – sometimes loving and sometimes cruel

behaves badly to Bertha, Céline Varens and others

Byronic hero – 'mad, bad and dangerous to know', but attractive

Rochester

Thornfield Hall is 'not vast, though considerable'

superior to Jane

wealthy

tries to buy Jane's affection

when he loses his sight, he becomes more equal – Jane rescues him

"I have a right to be a little masterful"

at the end of the novel, lives at Ferndean, a place of 'moderate size'

Activity 3

1. Use a spider diagram to plan an answer to each of the following questions:

   a) What is the significance of education in *Jane Eyre*?

   b) How is St. John Rivers presented in *Jane Eyre*?

2. Share your ideas with the rest of the class, then add any new ideas to your plan.

Tips for assessment

- Plan your time carefully in your assessment. Don't spend too long on your plan or you may run out of time to complete your answer.
- Don't cross out your plan because if you do run out of time you may be given credit for it.

Writing your answer

Once you have a good plan, you will have a clear idea of what you need to write and how to structure your ideas. When writing your answer, you should start with a brief introduction, develop your argument point by point, supported by references and short quotations, and finish with a conclusion that does not merely repeat the introduction, but takes it further.

For example, in the question about the presentation of Rochester on page 93:

- you could start with a brief introduction to Rochester's character at the beginning of the novel and how Brontë presents this
- your development could show how the characterization of Rochester changes as the novel progresses
- in the conclusion, you might suggest that the character of Rochester represents the idea that people can be redeemed if they atone for their sins.

Your answer should show your knowledge and understanding of:

- what the writer is saying
- how the writer is saying it
- how the setting and context influence the writer and reader (where relevant).

You also need to pay close attention to the quality of your writing, including your spelling, punctuation and grammar.

Using PEEE (Point, Evidence, Explanation, Effect)

You need to demonstrate that you can support your ideas in a thoughtful way and that you have based them on what the writer says and means. For example, you might make the point:

> Brontë presents Rochester as a Byronic hero.

Your evidence for this might be:

> She shows us this when she describes him as having 'a dark face with stern features' (Volume 1, Chapter 12).

Your explanation might be:

> This suggests that he is somehow mysterious and the word 'dark' suggests that he may also be threatening in some way.

Your comment on the effect might be:

> This makes the reader feel that he is someone who may bring danger into the story.

Tips for assessment

Upgrade

While PEEE is a helpful reminder of what you need to build into your writing, you do not need to follow this pattern for every single point you make. It is useful for the important points, but you should avoid getting bogged down with unnecessary repetition. To reach the higher grades, you need to control your argument and try to keep your answer flowing.

Using quotations

This is an important part of using evidence in your answer. You need to show that you can select appropriate quotations that back up the point you are making. When you make a point, ask yourself: 'How do I know this?' Usually it will be because of something the author has written – this is the quotation you need.

For example, you might make the point:

> Rochester is presented as a superior character who can sometimes treat others as though they are beneath him.

How do you know this? Well, there might be a number of quotations you could choose, but here is one:

> In Volume I, Chapter 14, he tells Jane that he thinks that he has a right to "be a little masterful" over her because he has "battled through a varied experience with many men of many nations".

By choosing this quotation you will show that you:

- can select a relevant quotation to support your answer
- have understood how to use quotations effectively as part of your sentences, rather than tacking them onto the end
- have understood that Rochester's view of the world is based only on his own experiences.

Tips for assessment

Upgrade

To show skills of a higher level, try to use embedded quotations. These short quotations (usually only a few words long) are easy to build into the flow of your own writing.

If you really want to use a long quotation for some reason, you need to mark it with speech marks and give it its own paragraph. But consider it carefully – usually a brief quotation is all that is needed and a long quotation takes up more of your writing time.

The extract

If you have to answer an extract question, remember that the extract has been chosen because there are lots of things that you can say about it when you answer the question. Here are some top tips to help you to answer an extract-based question effectively:

1. Read the question carefully.
2. Now read the extract carefully. As you do, highlight or underline any quotations that you might use in your answer and make quick notes in the margin. You might want to think about:
   - the language that is used

- the structure, e.g. How does the extract start and end?
- What new information does the extract reveal that we didn't know before this point in the story?
- How does Brontë reveal ideas about the context in the extract?
- How does the extract fit into the bigger picture of the text as a whole?

3. Re-read the question and check that your notes are helpful.

4. Write a quick plan, using your highlighting and notes to help you.

5. Now tackle the question.

> Explore how Brontë presents Jane's feelings for Mr Rochester in this extract. Give examples from the extract to support your ideas.

e has been waiting for ...n.

e can't keep her mind ... him.

e can't avoid thinking ...out him.

And where is Mr. Rochester?

He comes in last: I am not looking at the arch, yet I see him enter. I try to concentrate my attention on these netting-needles, on the meshes of the purse I am forming—I wish to think only of the work I have in my hands, to see only the silver beads and silk threads that lie in my lap; whereas, I distinctly behold his figure, and I inevitably recall the moment when I last saw it: just after I had rendered him, what he deemed, an essential service—and he, holding my hand, and looking down on my face, surveyed me with eyes that revealed a heart full and eager to overflow; in whose emotions I had a part. How near had I approached him at that moment! What had occurred since, calculated to change his and my relative positions? Yet now, how distant, how far estranged we were! So far estranged, that I did not expect him to come and speak to me. I did not wonder, when, without looking at me, he took a seat at the other side of the room, and began conversing with some of the ladies.

e can't keep her mind ... him.

..xtaposes her feelings: it's ...easure and pain because ...e wants him but she can't ...ve him.

No sooner did I see that his attention was riveted on them, and that I might gaze without being observed, than my eyes were drawn involuntarily to his face: I could not keep their lids under control: they would rise, and the irids would fix on him. I looked, and had an acute pleasure in looking,—a precious, yet poignant pleasure; pure gold, with a steely point of agony: a pleasure like what the thirst-perishing man might feel who knows the well to which he has crept is poisoned, yet stoops and drinks divine draughts nevertheless.

e knows that he is not ...nventionally attractive.

..mehow, he has control ...er her.

..e feels powerless to do ...ything about the way that ...e feels about him.

Most true is it that "beauty is in the eye of the gazer." My master's colourless, olive face, square, massive brow, broad and jetty eyebrows, deep eyes, strong features, firm, grim mouth, —all energy, decision, will,—were not beautiful, according to rule; but they were more than beautiful to me: they were full of an interest, an influence that quite mastered me,—that took my feelings from my own power and fettered them in his. I had not intended to love him: the reader knows I had wrought hard to extirpate from my soul the germs of love there detected; and now, at the first renewed view of him, they spontaneously revived, green and strong! He made me love him without looking at me.

Activity 4

1. Look at the sample questions on pages 99–100. If the questions are based around an extract from the novel, make sure that you read the extract carefully. Choose one sample question and create a plan for an answer using one of the methods on pages 92–94.

2. Share your ideas with a partner to check that you are working along the correct lines.

3. Now write your answer.

What not to do in an exam answer

✗ Do not begin with introductions such as 'In this essay I am going to...'. Instead just start straight in and do the showing as you go. Make sure your introduction addresses the question and that you go back to it in your conclusion.

✗ Do not write a long introduction showing what you know about the author. Make just a brief reference and only if it is relevant to a point you are making.

✗ Do not write lengthy paragraphs about the background to the novel. You may think that information about religion and social class are important in the novel, but show this briefly while you focus on answering the actual question.

✗ If you are responding to a set extract, do not answer on other parts of the novel, unless you are asked to do so.

✗ Do not focus on some parts of the set extract and ignore others. Always answer on the passage as a whole.

✗ Do not go into the exam with a prepared list of points and write about them, regardless of whether they are relevant to the question.

✗ Do not mention literary techniques the author has used in the set extract just for the sake of it. Only do so if you can show how she does this and what effects they create.

✗ Do not run out of time to finish your answer – a plan will help you avoid this. It is better to focus on a detailed answer on a small part of the text than to try to make lots of different points.

✗ Do not try to write everything you know about the text. Make sure that you only choose things that are relevant to the question.

Tips for assessment

Achieving the best marks

Upgrade

To achieve the highest marks, you will need to do the following:

- show an assured or perceptive understanding of themes/ideas
- show a pertinent or convincing response to the text
- select evidence that is relevant, detailed and sustained
- make references to context that are pertinent, convincing and supported by sustained relevant textual reference
- use sentences that are sophisticated and varied; show precise control of expression and meaning; use a full range of punctuation and spelling that is consistently accurate.

In practice this means that you need to read more than just the set text. Ideally you should read some critical guides to the text and add their interpretation to your own response and ideas about the book.

You need to show that you have understood the book on more than one level. On the surface, it is the story of one young woman's growing up and the events of a short period of her life. If you look more deeply, it is about women finding their identity and independence for themselves.

You will have to show that you understand the way in which the narrative works and why Brontë chose to have the story told by a narrator who is looking back on her childhood.

In addition you will need to use the correct literary terminology to make your answers more precise and show that you have a sophisticated writing style.

Sample questions

1

Read the extract from Volume 2, Chapter 8 which begins "I grieve to leave Thornfield" and ends "and we stood at God's feet, equal—as we are!" and then answer the question which follows:

Starting with this extract, how does Brontë present the differences between classes and genders?

Write about:

- how Brontë presents the differences between classes and genders in this extract
- how Brontë presents the differences between classes and genders in the novel as a whole.

2

Read the extract from Volume 1, Chapter 2 which begins 'Daylight began to forsake the red-room' and ends 'I rushed to the door and shook the lock in desperate effort'.

You should use the extract and your knowledge of the whole novel to answer this question.

Write about how a sense of fear and tension is created at different points in the novel.

In your response you should:
- refer to the extract and the novel as a whole
- show your understanding of characters and events in the novel
- refer to the contexts of the novel.

3

Choose ONE question. You are advised to spend about 45 minutes on this section.

EITHER

Read the extract from Volume 2, Chapter 3 which begins 'I saw he was going to marry her' and ends 'a silent conquest might have been won'.

Explore how Brontë presents ideas about love and marriage in this extract and elsewhere in the novel.

OR

'Jane spends most of the novel as an outsider.' How far do you agree with this view?

Explore at least two events from the novel to support your ideas.

4

Read the extract from Volume 1, Chapter 7 which begins "If people were always kind and obedient to those who are cruel and unjust" and ends "I live in calm, looking to the end."

a) Explore how Brontë presents what Jane thinks about how people who have mistreated her should be treated. Give examples from the extract to support your ideas.

b) In this extract, Jane Eyre thinks about how people who have mistreated her should be treated. Explain how and why she changes her views over the course of the novel. In your answer, you must consider:
- what the changes are
- what these show about her character.

Sample answers

Sample answer 1

Below you will find a sample answer from a student, together with examiner comments, to the following question on the novel:

Read the extract from Volume 3, Chapter 8 that begins "It is all very well for the present" and ends "forbear to waste them on trite transient objects".

Starting with this extract, how does Brontë present the idea of self-fulfilment in the novel?

Write about:
- how Brontë presents ideas about self-fulfilment in this extract
- how Brontë presents ideas about self-fulfilment in the novel as a whole.

Good to have a brief summary to begin with.

Accurate point with quotation. Could have been analysed in more detail.

Needs support.

Shows understanding of the context of the novel.

Moves beyond the extract to consider the rest of the novel. The point would have benefited from support with a quotation.

Effective analysis of the language used.

True but needs supporting with evidence.

Looks beyond the passage.

In this extract, Brontë presents the idea that people have very different ideas about what it means to be fulfilled. St. John's comment that "It is all very well for the present" makes it clear that he thinks that Jane should have greater aspirations for herself than arranging a house.

While Jane seems, in this passage, happy to content herself with a domestic life, his view is that this would not be fulfilling. In the Victorian period, women of Jane's class would not have generally worked outside the home, except as governesses or school mistresses, both of which Jane has been. She has previously found pleasure and self-fulfilment in these jobs, which suggests to the reader that she may not be being totally honest about being content with a domestic life.

When St. John describes life at Moor House as having the "selfish calm and sensual comfort of civilized affluence", these derogatory terms imply that he feels that anyone who considers themselves to be fulfilled by such things is both selfish and beneath his contempt. This, he reveals, is because of his religious convictions. He believes that in order to be able to please God, a person must struggle and overcome difficulty in life. His version of self-fulfilment relies a great deal on personal sacrifice.

This is also evident in his relationship with Rosamond Oliver. In Volume 1, Chapter 6, he claims to love her "wildy" and yet he will not marry her because "she would not make me a good wife". For St. John to achieve self-fulfilment, he will put aside his personal desires in order to do God's work. This attitude towards self-fulfilment contrasts sharply with Jane's view: whilst St. John will sacrifice himself to serve his God, Jane is unwilling to give up her own desires to suit other people.

Needs evidence.

Jane claims to be "disposed to be as content as a queen" yet she describes how 'hard I worked' readying the house for the arrival of Diana and Mary, stating that it 'was delightful' (Volume 3, Chapter 8). It is clear that she finds fulfilment in being occupied, despite St. John's belief that she should want to achieve more in her life.

Needs evidence.

To this end, he offers her the chance to join him in his missionary work, stating that she is "formed for labour, not for love" (Volume 3, Chapter 8). This attitude shows how strongly he feels that self-fulfilment can only come through doing God's work and not through personal relationships. While Jane believes that she "must seek another interest in life to replace the one lost: is not the occupation he now offers me truly the most glorious man can adopt or God assign? Is it not, by its noble cares and sublime results, the one best calculated to fill the void left by uptorn affections and demolished hopes?" (Volume 3, Chapter 8). It is clear that this approach would not be fulfilling her own desires. She recognizes the "glory" in the work that she would undertake and sees the value in carrying out God's work, but she is also aware that in doing so she would "abandon half myself" (Volume 3, Chapter 8). St. John's version of self-fulfilment involves sacrifice, whereas Jane's does not.

A long quotation that could have been looked at more closely.

Despite this, it is significant that she does not immediately reject the idea: she spends time considering the suggestion. This suggests that she has been influenced by his religious conviction and enables the reader to understand how much she has changed from the young girl who first met Helen Burns at Lowood. While she is now more able to see things from others' points of view, St. John's attitude is more single-minded: his only interest is his own self-fulfilment, even at the expense of others. His comment that if she "Refuse to be my wife, and you limit yourself for ever to a track of selfish ease and barren obscurity" (Volume 3, Chapter 8) reveals that he has little care for the needs or feelings of others, whereas Jane realizes that it would be 'unendurable' to be married to him, and that she could not provide him with the support that he needs.

Touches on structure but could have been developed further.

Needs further development.

Ultimately, both Jane and St. John find self-fulfilment; Jane as Rochester's wife and the mother of his child, and St. John as a missionary, devoted to God's work. However, Brontë reveals that St. John's fulfilment comes at a price – he will die young – suggesting perhaps that he was mistaken to believe that self-sacrifice could really lead to a fulfilling life. Jane, on the other hand, is presented as 'supremely blest' (Volume 3, Conclusion).

A nice quotation to end on, but needs more development.

This answer shows that the candidate knows the text well and can trace a theme through it. It begins with the extract and returns to it, but also ranges confidently around the novel. The candidate uses quotations to support their ideas but there are not enough of them. Some of the language used is analysed, but more thought needs to be given to specific choices made by Brontë.

Activity 5

Using the advice given above and what you know about *Jane Eyre*, rewrite this essay to make it better.

Sample answer 2

Read the extract from Volume 2, Chapter 2 that begins 'Then, in a lower tone' and ends "Am I right, Baroness Ingram of Ingram Park?"

You should use the extract and your knowledge of the whole novel to answer this question.

Write about how the importance of class is presented at different points in the novel.

In your response you should:
- refer to the extract and the novel as a whole
- show your understanding of characters and events in the novel
- refer to the contexts of the novel.

As a governess, Jane's position in society would have been an uncertain one. She is considered better than a mere servant, but not really a member of the household. The "her" that Lady Ingram refers to is, of course, Jane, and the fact that she is willing to speak in such a derogatory tone about her, knowing that she is near enough 'to hear', is indicative of Lady Ingram's attitude to class. Brontë doesn't tell the reader the tone, but we can infer it from what she is saying. She knows that she is superior to Jane and is happy to remind her of this at every possible opportunity. Jane herself is clearly conscious of this attitude, referring to herself as 'one of the anathematized race' (Volume 2, Chapter 2). This reminds the reader very clearly of the fact that this attitude was likely to have been prevalent at the time of the novel, with wealthy people relying on governesses to help bring up their children, but condemning the governesses nonetheless. Of course, Brontë's own experiences may have influenced her presentation of Lady Ingram's attitude here.

Lady Ingram's suggestion that Jane's appearance shows "all the faults of her class" is suggestive of a view that "her class" is inferior. This is a view shared by her daughter, who refers to them as a "tribe" and a "nuisance". This choice of language seems significant. "Tribe" is suggestive of a savage and uncivilized group of the kind that St. John Rivers must bring to Christianity and evokes the idea that governesses and those of their class are not only inferior to the upper classes, but also of an entirely different species. When she describes them as a "nuisance", this reduces them almost to the status of children – to be suffered.

Begins with the context and sets the scene effectively.

The very short embedded quotation is effective.

Reads between the lines.

Looks outside the set extract. Another useful embedded quotation.

Links the point effectively to the reader.

Context – this feels a little like an afterthought – could be linked in a little more smoothly.

Developed analysis of language.

Makes links outside the extract.

Analytical.

Analyses some of the language of the text in a focused and effective way.

Makes effective links with other parts of the text.

When Blanche describes how, as a child, she treated her own governesses, she states that they were "merry days". It is clear that she, and perhaps by extension others of her class, consider that mistreating governesses is par for the course: they are of a lower class and are therefore not considered to be worthy of being treated as decent human beings. This is, of course, similar to the way in which Jane is treated by John Reed earlier in the novel when he describes her as a "dependant". Because she is of a lower social status, she is treated with contempt.

Develops the idea with references from elsewhere in the text.

Lord Ingram seems to revel in this mistreatment of the lower social orders, referring to his mistreated governess as a "poor old stick" and commenting that she was presumptuous to attempt "to teach such clever blades as we were". This reveals an arrogant attitude to the lower classes. They are also referred to as "dead-weights" which again reveals a supercilious attitude: Blanche does not value the contribution that these women have made to her upbringing. This belief that they have nothing to offer is reiterated later when Lady Ingram says that Jane "looks too stupid for any game" of cards (Volume 2, Chapter 3).

An embedded quotation would have been more effective.

When Blanche comments on the problems associated with governesses, she seems to be suggesting that they are morally bankrupt: "danger of bad example to innocence of childhood". Once again, this is suggestive of a complete ignorance of the benefits that having a governess offers. Blanche's view is entirely based on her prejudices about the lower classes, and she is incapable of seeing their strengths. This is reinforced when she refers to her mother as "Baroness Ingram of Ingram Park". It is highly unlikely that this is her normal term of address towards her mother, which suggests that there is a more unpleasant purpose behind her choice of words. She is aware that she can be overheard by Jane, and it seems likely that this is a pointed remark, made in order to remind the lowly governess of her inferior position.

Develops beyond the extract to comment on other attitudes to class.

Links effectively to context.

This arrogance is not limited to the wealthy commenting on their governesses, however. Jane herself reveals a negative attitude towards those in classes lower than herself, with a view that the poor are collectively a "beggarly set" (Volume 1, Chapter 3). This attitude is likely to have been common at the time, with people generally having little informed understanding of the ways in which people in other classes lived their lives. It is notable, however, that – as an adult – she comments that 'poverty looks grim to grown people' (Volume 1, Chapter 3). This perhaps reveals that Jane has continued to develop over the course of the novel due to her experiences and that this has enabled her to have a more rounded view of the world in which she lives: something which people of the upper social classes are unable, or perhaps unwilling, to do.

It is also the case that judgements about class are made by the lower classes towards those they consider to be inferior. In Volume 1, Chapter 6, Mrs Fairfax advises Jane not to "converse with [the other servants] on terms of equality" for "fear of losing one's authority". This reminds the reader that even within the serving classes, there was a hierarchy in which housekeepers and governesses were superior to domestic servants. Her comment that "Leah is a nice girl" and "John and his wife are very decent people" is suggestive of an attitude of surprise that people she considers her social inferiors are "nice". This is perhaps indicative of a wider belief that the lower classes are unlikely to be pleasant or decent.

Reference to other issues of class from elsewhere in the novel.

It is clear, therefore, that class is a vitally important aspect of the novel. All of the classes have views of the other classes which are based on generalizations which they seem to be reluctant to give up.

Sums up effectively.

This answer is effectively written and shows that the candidate is able to make connections and trace ideas across the whole text. They make good points that are well supported with evidence. Consideration is given to the context in an effective way, linking it closely and carefully to aspects of the text.

Sample answer 3

> 'Brontë presents Rochester as an unpleasant character who does not deserve Jane's love.' How far do you agree with this view?
>
> Explore at least two events from the novel to support your ideas.

Makes good use of quotation.

Clear awareness of a writer at work.

Considers reader response.

Looks at different sections of the novel; needs more development for clearer explanation.

Considers context.

Considers reader response.

From the first time that we are introduced to Rochester, he is presented as mysterious and threatening, with his 'stern features and a heavy brow' (Volume 1, Chapter 12). On Jane's first formal meeting with him, he is presented as rather ignorant in that he 'neither spoke nor moved' (Volume 1, Chapter 13). Brontë presents him as choosing not to put Jane, his new governess, at her ease and that suggests to the reader that he may be a dislikeable character, despite the fact that Jane has already alluded to their 'romance' (Volume 1, Chapter 12). Of course, it would probably have been common for masters to choose not to interact a great deal with the servants, and especially not with the governess, but this seems to the reader to be indicative of an unpleasant facet to his character.

This point needs to be developed more fully.

Colloquial and needs more support with quotation.

Considers reader response.

When he does talk to Jane, it is immediately clear that he finds her interesting: he asks her questions that she answers honestly and that cause Mrs Fairfax some surprise. This suggests that his attitude to her is different to his customary attitude to servants, but he also orders her about. This seemingly inconsistent way of treating her might suggest that he doesn't really know how to behave around her – but it is also an example of the sometimes unpleasant way in which he treats her. In Volume 1, Chapter 13, he goes from barely speaking to her at all, to ordering her around, to complimenting her on her painting, and then dismisses her from the room 'abruptly'. This causes Jane to comment that he "is very changeful and abrupt". While some people would find this uncomfortable or even unpleasant, Jane notes that 'his changes of mood did not offend' her. Although this suggests that she does not think him unpleasant, this is a facet of his character that the reader might not judge kindly, and suggests that Brontë wanted the reader to understand these seeming contradictions.

Despite this, though, there are elements of his character that are clearly kind. Adèle Varens is "Mr. Rochester's ward" and he clearly provides for her very well in terms of material possessions and affection. This contrasts sharply with the way in which Jane was cared for by the Reeds and reminds the reader that not every character has the same capacity for kindness that Rochester does. It is important to remember, however, that his relationship with Céline (and his other mistresses) was carried out whilst he was married to Bertha Mason and had her confined in the attics of his house. This shows another, less desirable, side to his character, which makes him – in my view – unworthy of Jane's love.

Considers reader response.

Clear personal response links effectively back to the question.

When Jane rebels against his desire to shower her with expensive gifts, she tells him that she "will not be your English Céline Varens" (Volume 2, Chapter 9), suggesting that she, too, sees aspects of his character that she does not like. She also alludes to this again after the revelation of his marriage: "I don't like you so well as I have done sometimes" (Volume 3, Chapter 1), but it is notable that she still loves him. It is clear that she differentiates between her liking of him, which seems to relate to her response to how she is treated and how he treats others, and her love of him, which never wavers. It is because she loves him that she is able to forgive him 'at the moment, and on the spot' (Volume 3, Chapter 1) regardless of his treatment of others. She commented much earlier in the novel that 'I had learnt to love Mr. Rochester: I could not unlove him now' (Volume 2, Chapter 3).

Makes an interesting distinction.

Ranges confidently around the text.

She does, however, remonstrate with him over his attitude to his wife, noting that he is "inexorable for that unfortunate lady: you speak of her with hate—with vindictive antipathy. It is cruel—she cannot help being mad" (Volume 3, Chapter 1). Here Brontë shows us that, despite Jane's love of him, she is not blind to his faults. Some people might argue that the loss of his home and his sight is an adequate punishment for his actions and that, in the end, he is redeemed by his love for Jane, but I do not agree. The way in which he treats Bertha, and the fact that he is prepared to marry Jane bigamously, shows that he puts himself and his own desires above those of others, making him deeply unpleasant.

When he tells her that "so long as my visitors stay, I expect you to appear in the drawing room every evening: it is my wish; don't neglect it" this shows that he puts his own desires and wishes above those of other people. As her master, he has every right to tell Jane what to do, but this does not mean that he should treat her in such a dismissive way.

Links to context.

It is also true that he treats Jane badly over the issue of his engagement to Blanche Ingram. Jane sees immediately that 'he was going to marry her, for family, perhaps political reasons; because her rank and connexions suited him' (Volume 2, Chapter

3). It is soon clear to the reader, although perhaps not to Jane, that Rochester has no intention of marrying Blanche and that he is merely toying with her affections at the same time as toying with Jane's. Again, this reveals a side to his character that is unpleasant. While the reader is intended to sympathize with Jane, we also find ourselves sympathizing – to a lesser extent – with Blanche. Despite the fact that she is clearly only interested in Rochester for his status, he has treated her unfairly.

An interesting point which shows clear engagement with the details of the text.

In Volume 3, Chapter 11, when Jane returns to Rochester at the end of the novel, he reveals that he has lived a "dark, dreary, hopeless life" without her and Jane notes that he is like 'a lamp quenched, waiting to be relit'. She clearly feels compassion for him in his misery, but readers may feel that he has deserved to suffer for his actions. His 'jealousy' over Jane's relationship with St. John Rivers is well deserved after his treatment of her in the past, but this shows the true depth of his feelings for her. When they are married, she describes how he is 'what I love best on earth' (Volume 3, Conclusion). She clearly feels that he is worthy of her love, but a modern reader especially must wonder whether this is true.

Makes a suitably tentative response.

Makes an interesting point which could have been developed further.

Rochester is, of course, a typical Byronic hero: 'mad, bad and dangerous to know', and in spite of this, or maybe because of it, a deeply attractive character to some.

The question does not direct the student to a specific extract and the answer ranges confidently around the text. It is well supported with a range of quotations and some consideration is given to the context, although this could have been developed more clearly. There are some points about language, but these needed to be developed more fully.

Activity 6

Using the advice given above and what you know about *Jane Eyre*, rewrite this essay to make it better.

Practising exam-style questions

Upgrade

One of the best ways to prepare for the exam is by looking closely at and practising how you will answer the types of question that will appear. Look closely at example questions for the exam, and write your own in a similar style. If you work with a partner, you can then have a go at answering one another's questions.

Glossary

accomplishments pastimes, such as painting, singing, dancing, playing the piano and speaking a foreign language, considered desirable for a young lady

allude to refer to something indirectly

apothecary a type of doctor who treated people for free

atone make amends

autobiography literally means 'writing the self'; a true account of someone's life from their own point of view

barbarous cruel

bequeath to leave someone something when you die

bigamy being married to more than one person at the same time

Bildungsroman a coming-of-age novel in which the main character grows up and develops moral judgement

binary opposites things which are totally opposite, for example, hot and cold

boarders students who stayed overnight at the school, as well as going for lessons

Byronic hero a type of male character created by Lord Byron who is typically brooding, rebellious and darkly romantic

Calvinist a set of Christian beliefs based on the teachings of John Calvin. Calvinism stresses the moral weakness of humans

caricature a description in which certain features are exaggerated to make them appear ridiculous

chronological arranged in the order of time in which events occurred

cipher *(or cypher)* to solve basic maths problems

class the social group that people belonged to

clause a part of a sentence which makes sense on its own

clergyman a priest or vicar in the Christian Church

coercion pressure

complicit part of; an accomplice

corporal punishment being caned or smacked

denomination a religious group with a recognized name

doctrines rules

dowry money paid by the father of the bride to the groom when a couple marry

Edenic a paradise, like the biblical Garden of Eden

election the idea that God chooses people to be saved based on whether He thinks they will have religious faith

elysium the dwelling place of the blessed after death in Greek mythology; a place of perfect bliss

eponymous the person the novel is named after

estate a person's assets, for example their property and money

Evangelical movement a religious movement that tries to convert others to its faith

fallacy false or mistaken belief

familial relating to family

fiancé the man a woman is engaged to marry

figurative language words or expressions with a meaning that is different from the literal interpretation

first person a story written from the viewpoint of a character writing or speaking directly about themselves using 'I'

foil a character whose role is to highlight some aspect of another character's attitudes or beliefs

foreshadowed hinted at

genre a literary category such as comedy, tragedy, romance

gothic a type of fiction that includes references to death and fear, but also to nature and emotion

governess a woman employed by a wealthy family to educate their children in their own home

graven image a carved idol used as an object of worship

Hindostanee the language of North India and Pakistan

hypocritical pretending to be good, moral or honourable but never actually demonstrating these qualities

imagery the use of visual or other vivid language to convey ideas or emotions

immorality wicked behaviour

incarcerated imprisoned

Industrial Revolution the period from about 1760 when goods began to be made in factories, giving many more people the opportunity for employment

infidelity unfaithfulness

inheritance the property, money and title of a person who dies, which can be given to someone else

injudicious careless and badly informed

irony words that express the opposite of what is meant

John the Baptist a distinctive and fearless preacher in the time of Jesus, who believed unfailingly in his religious mission. He was beheaded by Herod Antipas

metaphor a comparison of one thing to another to make a description more vivid; unlike a simile, it does not use the words 'like' or 'as'

missionary member of a religious group that spreads the teachings of that religion in another country

mistress teacher

morality right and wrong, acting according to principle

motif a word or phrase or image repeated during the course of the novel

narrative perspective the position from which the story is told

narrator the person telling the story

onomatopoeia where the sound of the word suggests its meaning

oppression using power to put other people down

pathetic fallacy where nature suggests human emotions or sympathies

pathos a quality that causes the reader to feel sympathy and sadness

paysannes French peasant women

philanthropic charitable work, such as teaching in Sunday school. This work was often linked to religious organizations

pious religious

predestination the idea that God has already chosen some people to be saved, and that nothing can change that

proleptic forecasting the future; another word for foreshadowing

protagonist main character

pseudonym a 'pen name'; the name a writer uses so they don't have to use their real name

redeem save from the consequences of sin, or make up for faults

rendered made

repentance feeling of regret

reprobation those who are not chosen will not be saved and will therefore be damned

retrospective looking back

sentimental novel a type of fiction written to evoke an emotional response

supernatural ghosts and other creatures that do not belong to the natural world

symbol a word which has a literal meaning but also another meaning of wider significance, representing an idea or concept

sympathetic character someone the reader can feel sympathy for or care about

tenet firm belief or principle

third person from the perspective of a character or voice outside the story, using the pronouns 'he' or 'she'

tuberculosis a highly infectious disease characterized by excessive and persistent coughing

unbiased balanced viewpoint, fair and accurate

unreliable narrator a first-person narrator who sometimes fails to tell the truth or recount events accurately, allowing a reader to draw their own conclusions

vale of tears the trials of life Christians leave behind when they enter Heaven

ward the child that she is responsible for

OXFORD
UNIVERSITY PRESS

Great Clarendon Street, Oxford, OX2 6DP, United Kingdom

Oxford University Press is a department of the University of Oxford. It furthers the University's objective of excellence in research, scholarship, and education by publishing worldwide. Oxford is a registered trade mark of Oxford University Press in the UK and in certain other countries

© Alison Smith 2016

British Library Cataloguing in Publication Data

Data available

ISBN 978-019-835529-8

10 9 8 7 6 5 4 3 2 1

Printed in Great Britain by Bell and Bain Ltd., Glasgow

Acknowledgements
Cover: Jeff Wasserman/Shutterstock; **p6:** Moviestore Collection/ REX Shutterstock; **p10:** © Underwood & Underwood/Corbis; **p18:** Moviestore/REX Shutterstock; p24: ITV/REX Shutterstock; **p30:** Snap Stills/REX Shutterstock; **p36:** © The Print Collector/Alamy; **p37:** © The Print Collector/Alamy; **p40:** © Stapleton Collection/Corbis; **p42:** © Wolverhampton City Council - Arts and Heritage/Alamy; **p44:** © AF archive/Alamy; **p46:** ITV/REX Shutterstock; **p52:** Snap Stills/REX Shutterstock; **p56:** Moviestore/REX Shutterstock; **p62:** Alastair Muir/ REX Shutterstock; **p64:** © Photos 12/Alamy; **p70:** © Mark Forster/ Snapwire/Corbis; **p72:** Amy Johansson/Shutterstock; **p75:** © LOOK Die Bildagentur der Fotografen GmbH/Alamy; **p78:** © Heritage Image Partnership Ltd/Alamy; **p85:** © Fred de Noyelle/Godong/Corbis; **p88:** Snap Stills/REX Shutterstock;

Extracts are taken from Charlotte Brontë: *Jane Eyre* edited by Margaret Smith (Oxford World Classics, 2008).

MIX
Paper from
responsible sources
FSC
www.fsc.org
FSC® C007785